Happy Ch[ristmas]
— I know [ther]e
is no ~~~ be
this will be useful
at sometime in the
future — maybe when
you retire !!!

With love
[Pam] & Bill

Xmas 1992

THE ORGANIC
GARDEN
DOCTOR

JACKIE FRENCH

THE ORGANIC GARDEN DOCTOR

ANGUS
& ROBERTSON
PUBLISHERS

ANGUS & ROBERTSON PUBLISHERS

Unit 4, Eden Park, 31 Waterloo Road,
North Ryde, NSW, Australia 2113, and
16 Golden Square, London W1R 4BN,
United Kingdom

First published in Australia
by Angus & Robertson Publishers in 1988
Published by arrangement with
Bacragas Pty Ltd

Copyright © Jacqueline French

ISBN 0 207 16039 2

Typeset in 12pt Garamond Light Condensed
by The Typeshop Pty Limited
Printed by Owen King Printers Pty Ltd, Victoria

CONTENTS

INTRODUCTION

Organic gardening is a natural way of gardening. More and more people are questioning the effort which transforms a garden into a barren wonderland where no insect, bird, butterfly or small animal is safe from the harmful effects of chemicals.

Organic gardeners want to enjoy nature — isn't that the point of having a garden? Every insect is not an enemy but rather food for a lizard or fairy wren. We tolerate the occasional chewed leaf or damaged flower to ensure that birds are regular visitors. Aphids may multiply on roses for a week or two, but it is not long before ladybirds arrive to feast off them. That's the best way to deal with any pest; it is natural, requires no work and costs no money.

In an organic garden there is no health risk and no destruction of the environment. Organically grown vegetables are rich in vitamins and minerals and guaranteed to be spray-free. Nevertheless, it is not always a Garden of Eden. A plant may fail because the soil lacks the right minerals or a minor horde of insects may need discouraging. The answer is not an arsenal of potent chemicals, but the dozens of gentler organic methods which keep the soil and plants healthy.

This book outlines many of the safe, natural methods that can be used to deal with common garden problems.

TOWARDS A HEALTHY
GARDEN

Organic gardening is about growing things, not killing things. Pest and disease problems are usually the result of human mismanagement. We destroy natural, varied plant communities, we use pesticides that destroy natural predators, introduce exotic pests that don't have native predators and use high nitrogen fertilisers which promote soft, sappy growth. All these and other bad management practices can lead to uncontrollable pest and disease problems.

There are gardeners who race for the spray can at the first sight of an insect, others take action only when they see that pest actually damaging the plants. On the other hand, there are those who tolerate the damage as long as possible, waiting for natural predators or good growing techniques to solve their problems for them. These gardeners may not have model gardens by conventional standards — there may be holes in the cabbage leaves, black spot on the roses — but their gardens will almost certainly be productive, happy and safe for children and animals.

This is a book of common garden problems and shows how to deal with them organically without resorting to harmful pesticides, herbicides, fungicides or soil sterilants. Plants have grown, seeded and fruited for thousands of years without human assistance. It's time we watched and learnt from them. But there are a number of steps that should be followed to ensure a healthy garden.

Encourage predators, especially birds, by planting flowering shrubs and annuals — always have something going to seed. Create plenty of hiding places in your garden for lizards and frogs; provide water for the birds; discourage dogs and cats which will keep these predators from the open areas of your garden.

Wherever possible, avoid pesticides. Every pest you kill means less food for a predator, discouraging them from visiting your garden. Once you spray — even with an organic pesticide that breaks down quickly — you may have to keep on spraying to prevent a population explosion of pests as they become more and more resistant to the pesticide. If you must, use the gentler pesticides and fungicides such as onion spray, soapy water or chamomile tea, before trying a bordeaux mixture, pyrethrum or garlic spray. Specific remedies should be used first to keep the problem down to manageable levels before calling all out war with the more general pesticides.

Don't see every insect as an enemy. Some insects benefit plants directly, others clear up pests and any insect is either a predator of your pests or food for them. All are to be cherished until damage to your crop makes control, not elimination, a necessity. Avoid high nitrogen artificial fertilisers which promote soft, sappy growth that attracts pests and diseases. Organic growing is based on the slow, steady release of nutrients from organic matter such as mulch, green manure and compost. Let the life in your soil be as rich as the life above it with micro-organisms that will either inhibit pathogens or increase your plant's resistance to them. Dig as little as possible and leave organic material on the soil's surface to rot naturally or be pulled under by earthworms and other foragers.

Strongly growing plants are more resistant to pests and disease, therefore, it is essential to feed your plants properly and watch their water requirements. Energy spent on pest control could be better spent tending the plants.

Many organic remedies that are poisonous to pests are also poisonous to beneficial organisms like bees and lacewings and even to human beings. If you must store them, label the container **Poison** and keep it out of the reach of children, but use at once if possible.

Organic pesticides break down quickly and for this reason must be used more frequently than conventional controls. People complain that many of the remedies don't work, not realising that they have been effective, but the plant has become reinfested. If a plant is continually diseased or pest prone, be ruthless. It may be unsuitable for your area — or a poor cultivar. Keep your own seed from well adapted plants, take cuttings from neighbour's gardens but, as far as possible, avoid greenhouse plants grown outside your district.

Don't have unrealistic expectations. Some pest infestation is inevitable — and desirable. Don't apologise for the caterpillar holes in your cabbage leaves, without pests there can be no predators — and your crops can be devastated by the next pest to be introduced. Plant extra, if necessary, to feed the birds. Treat them as welcome guests.

Many of the remedies in this book can be used for more than one pest or disease. If you can't identify a pest, try to identify the damage it is doing. If it seems to be sucking sap, if leaves are mottled or new shoots wilt, try the remedies suggested for aphids or red spider mite. If the leaves are chewed, look up caterpillars or beetles or bugs. If you have no idea what is harming your plant and action must be taken, mix up a pyrethrum spray with chamomile tea and seaweed spray. Spray in the evening under the leaves as well as on top, then try to identify your problem so you can take specific action.

The best gardening technique is almost instinctive — a gentle touch to correct a problem before the worst symptoms appear. Complete plant foods, specific herbicides, all purpose rose dusts or azalea sprays are easy to use, but you lose the joy of understanding your garden and being part of its processes. Most of the solutions given in this book don't involve sprays at all and if they do, they are mostly homemade. Use the bought remedies recommended if you must.

This is a book for gardeners who love and try to understand their gardens. The more you learn to adapt to the processes of your garden the less you'll find pest and disease control necessary.

BENEFICIAL GARDEN PREDATORS

No matter how much of an ecological desert your suburb may seem to be, there will be some predators there. The trick is to recognise and encourage them.

A couple of years ago I grew 2000 cauliflowers, and with them came the cabbage-white butterflies and their leaf-eating offspring. If I had sprayed the caterpillars, even with an organic remedy like derris or Dipel, I would probably have had to continue doing so until the crop had matured. I squashed the caterpillars by hand and left them on the leaves. After about ten days there were munched leaves but no caterpillars, and soon after that a steady stream of wasps and yellow robins were harvesting what I regarded as a pest and they thought of as dinner. The butterflies kept laying, the caterpillars kept hatching, the predators kept eating — and I was finally able to harvest unblemished cauliflowers.

This is natural pest control. You don't get a good population of beneficial predators unless you have pests for them to eat — the secret is to keep the pests within reasonable bounds while the predator population builds up.

Unfortunately, natural pest control is not as easy to achieve in the suburban garden. I had bush around the paddock in which the cauliflowers were planted and many other species growing nearby: in the suburbs there is not the same diversity. Pests and predators alike are wiped out by zealous insect exterminators who cannot tell one from the other and by neighbourhood dogs and cats that kill or discourage birds, frogs and lizards which eat so many garden pests.

Here is a list of the most common predators. Do not underestimate their value.

Ant lions

Their larvae eat a wide range of ground-based insects.

Ants

These feed on many insects, particularly caterpillars and their larvae, and fruit-fly maggots in the soil. Use grease-bands to prevent them from climbing up plants; otherwise, leave them alone.

Assassin bugs

These eat beetles, grasshoppers and caterpillars.

Birds

Watch them and remember which bird eats what. I have watched a kookaburra eat nine snails on my front lawn in the morning while I had my breakfast. Even nectar-eaters will prey on insects while they are nesting, so it is worthwhile attracting them to the garden. Yellow robins eat pear and cherry slug caterpillars, codling moth and cabbage-white butterfly larvae. Wattle birds and honeyeaters are voracious eaters of caterpillars. Black cockatoos eat wood-borers; magpies and curra-wongs eat snails, and so the list goes on. Most of our bird life is native, so be sure to have some native shrubs and flowers to attract them year-round. Keep cats out of the garden and provide the birds with thick bushes for shelter and shallow dishes of water high off the ground.

Beetles

Adults and their larvae feed on slugs, snails, snail eggs, mites, cutworm and moth larvae.

Centipedes

These eat caterpillars, slugs and other pests. They have only one leg per segment of the body. Don't squash them or confuse them with millipedes which have more than one leg per segment and chew plant leaves. Squash *them* if necessary.

Damsel bugs

The nymphs and adults eat large quantities of aphids and other sap-suckers.

Earwigs

These feed on detritus and small insects and their larvae, such as codling moth.

Frogs and toads

These eat insects, slugs and snails.

Hoverflies

These are probably the best predators to encourage for aphids, scale insects and mites. Their small larvae seem to like young cater-pillars, and pear and cherry slugs. Attract them to the garden by planting spring-flowering annuals and grevilleas. They like brassica and buckwheat flowers, and parsnips and radishes which are going to seed.

Lacewings

You can recognise lacewings by their trans-parent, metallic-looking wings. The adults and larvae eat aphids, scale insects, mealy bugs, mites, whitefly, thrips, pear and cherry slugs and I have even seen them dealing with codling moth larvae.

Ladybirds

Treasure all ladybirds except the 28-spot ones which eat potato and tomato foliage. Some species of ladybirds eat aphids, including woolly ones, thrips, mealy bugs, red spider and other mites, and scale insects. If you are prone to infestation by scale insects on new growth in spring and need to spray to control them, do it carefully. Spray alternate trees with white oil or bordeaux in winter, and the remaining ones 10 days later. This method makes sure the ladybirds are not wiped out and allows time for the population to build up for spring when you need most help with the scale insects.

Lizards

These eat slugs, snails, flies and, depending on their type, other insects. Provide some thick bush and rocks where they can hide, and keep cats out of the garden.

Praying mantids and their larvae

These eat aphids, caterpillars, hard-bodied beetles and other insects. They look a bit like locusts but lift their strong forelegs into the 'praying' position which immediately identifies them.

Robber or assassin flies

These will eat any insect they can catch.

Soldier beetles

These are brownish red or yellow and eat

codling moth larvae and other larvae. The adults like flowers.

Wasps

Many species of wasp prey on or parasitise pests. Not all of them sting, so do not reach for the aerosol can as soon as you see one around. Wasps eat the caterpillars of the cabbage-white butterfly, pear and cherry slug and codling moth. Some species of wasp parasitise beetles, mealy bugs, scale insects, caterpillars and a number of other pests. The chalcid wasp is small and coloured a metallic blue, black or brown. The flower wasp parasitises scarab beetle larvae.

Pest control is less a matter of killing off the pests than of making sure plants are growing strongly enough to withstand mild depredation while the beneficial predators in the area build up their numbers and take over the job. If you feed the plants, make sure you supply potash and phosphorus as well as nitrogen. A fertiliser too high in nitrogen will promote soft, sappy growth which pests love.

ENRICHING THE SOIL

Green manures

Green manures are crops which are grown solely for the purpose of enriching the soil; they are either dug in, or slashed and left on top of the soil to rot naturally. In these days of artificial fertilisers they are not used as often as they could be. Sandy or clay soils need the humus supplied by a green manure crop. A humus-rich soil is able both to retain moisture and to allow it to penetrate deeply. It has sufficient trace elements and can improve resistance to pathogen build-up.

Bare soil can be further denuded by wind and water, but if you plant a quick-growing crop such as mustard, radish or sunflowers to protect the soil until you are ready to use it, you will have food for the soil too. The crop will also prevent the build-up of weeds and use up excess nitrogen in the soil. A crop of mustard dug into the soil between early and late potato crops will deter the potato eelworm; oats and barley control root-knot eelworm.

The classic green manure crops are legumes; the bacteria associated with them fix nitrogen in the soil. One year's crop of legumes can convert 150 kg of airborne nitrogen per hectare for use in the soil; a crop of barley or buckwheat will increase the phosphorus available to the crop that follows them. Deep-rooted crops draw up nutrients from levels shallower-rooted crops cannot reach and, when they are used as green manure, make available nutrients which otherwise would be lost.

These plants can be used as green manure:

Borage

This is a fast grower and an excellent forager for leached nutrients.

Broad beans

These are nitrogen-fixers and produce a good quantity of organic matter. They should be planted in autumn and dug into the ground in early spring to provide food for the summer crops. Sow the seed thickly, about 5 cm deep using 5 grams of seed to the square metre. They will need feeding. If you want a summer or winter crop of broad beans for green manure you will not have any trouble; the beans will not set seed in heat or frost unless they are protected. Slash them just as the first flowers are falling.

Buckwheat

If planted in spring, buckwheat will flower and be ready for slashing six weeks later. Sow thickly, about 10 grams per square metre, and rake it in. It chokes out weeds, loosens heavy or clay soil, grows on the poorest soil and does not need feeding. It draws calcium and phosphorus up from the soil, making them readily available to the crops that follow.

Clover

Clover helps to aerate the soil, fixes nitrogen in it and, if you dig it in before it flowers, breaks down easily. However, it is hard to get rid of and can need an inoculant.

Lupins

These fix nitrogen in the soil and produce a quantity of organic matter. They will grow in both acid and alkaline soil, provided the drainage is good. They make phosphorus in the soil readily available to crops that follow. They can be planted in pure sand and, by repeated cropping and, digging in or slashing and leaving to rot, will turn the sand into soil. To do all this they do need to be inoculated with the right strain of bacteria. Buy the inoculant from the seed company which supplied the seed. Sow in April at about 15 grams of seed to a square metre of soil, and dig in just as the first flowers are showing in spring. Sowing may be done in spring, in which case they will be dug in during midsummer, but be alert, as at this time of year they are more susceptible to weeds and disease.

Marigolds

Dug in or slashed and left to decompose, these will help to control various nematodes.

Mustard

This makes a good green manure crop as long as you remember that it belongs to the brassica family and do not grow it either before or after any other member of the same family in the same plot. Mustard attracts cabbage-white butterflies. Sow it in spring, at about one gram per square metre; it will be ready in six to eight weeks. A crop grown between early and late potatoes will help to control potato eelworm. Mustard has slightly alkaline root secretions which are good for acid soil.

Oats

These help to control root-knot eelworm. They like acid soil and if you give them a high-nitrogen booster they will store nitrates for release for later crops. Sow 10 grams to the square metre in autumn and spring, or sow in spring and slash in midsummer. Always slash as the heads are starting to form. They need feeding if you are to get a good crop and must be irrigated in dry weather.

Peas

You can use either garden peas or field peas, which are grown as stock food. They are nitrogen-fixers and produce a fair amount of organic matter. They may need inoculating. Sow at about 15 grams to the square metre in spring for December crops and in autumn for spring crops. Slash when the plants are in flower.

Radish

This can be sown and used as a green manure at any time of year, depending on the variety. You can plant radish between rows of crops that are nearing maturity — the radish will be ready when the crop is picked and the residue of both can either be dug into the soil or slashed and left to rot on top of it.

Rye

This grows reasonably well without added fertiliser. Its deep roots bring up nutrients which would otherwise be leached away. It produces a good quantity of organic matter and is very good for keeping down invading grass and chickweed. Sow in autumn and slash in spring, just before the heads appear.

Sunflowers

A great deal of organic matter can be supplied by sunflowers. Sow them thickly in spring and slash before the flowers form while the stems are still tender and foliage soft.

Green manuring is a way of speeding up the natural process of soil creation and of time-tabling it to fit in with your cropping schedule.

Compost

Compost is manure made from vegetable matter — animal manure and rock dusts can be added to it. You can use compost as a fertiliser, as a mulch, or even as the sole growing medium to replace soil in a no-dig garden.

A compost heap is a pile of rotting layers of organic materials — garden waste, manure, soil or paper. Anything that rots can be composted. A good compost heap is a dynamic living body, a mass of bacteria, actinomycetes and fungi, all busy breaking down the plant fibre, bones and other components.

Compost is cheap; it recycles nutrients that might otherwise be lost. It encourages earthworms, can neutralise excess acid or alkali, may provide spores, living bacteria and fungi that suppress pathogens such as phytophthera root rot, eelworms and potato scurf, or supply fungal spores for mycorrhizal associations that help plants to develop a better resistance to disease. Inorganic plant nutrients such as phosphorus and potassium are released by the organic acids produced by the micro-organisms in compost. A good hot heap will help to control plant disease and kill off weed seeds.

You can make compost either with air — aerobic compost — or without it — anaerobic compost.

Aerobic compost

Most aerobic composts are the same as, or variations of, the classic Indore compost developed by Sir Albert Howard at Indore in India. When making the compost you must supply four basic needs: moisture, heat, nitrogen and air. The heap must be kept moist but not wet, and it should never get cold. If you shred all green waste before adding it to the pile you will speed the process.

A classic compost heap

Drive a stake into the ground. Remove the soil around it, or sprinkle some old compost over the soil. This is done to facilitate the entry of natural 'starters' present in soil or compost.

Pile the coarsest material you have over the soil to the circumference of the heap you propose to make. Branches or cornstalks are excellent. Cover it with a handspan depth of green garden waste. Scatter over it some nitrogenous matter, such as blood and bone, old dried hen manure or human urine. If you have cow manure you can use a little more of that. Add another layer of green matter, a layer of kitchen scraps, then a thin layer of soil. Continue adding in the same sequence and, if you can, make the pile in one go.

Add water and turn the pile with a fork every three to four days, adding more water if it seems dry. If it does not heat up after a week, add some more nitrogenous matter or water it with green liquid manure. The compost should be ready in six weeks.

Two week compost

Chop up or shred vegetable matter or garden waste using a shredder, mower or garden shears. Make a pile about a metre high and wide. Moisten it with liquid green manure. Turn the compost every two days, adding more liquid manure if it seems too dry. If it fails to begin to heat after two days add some stronger liquid manure. The secret of this method is the frequent turning, the finely chopped ingredients and the high nitrogen level.

Pit compost

The advantage of a pit compost heap is that it is unobtrusive; on the other hand it takes work to dig the pit and nutrients can leach away and be lost.

Dig the pit about a metre square so that you can reach into it easily. Drive a stake into the middle of the pit. Make a bottom layer of old branches, cornstalks, or any coarse matter and cover it with a layer of garden waste about 20-25 cm deep. Add a layer of old hen manure, a few centimetres deep, or a sprinkling of blood and bone, then continue alternating a layer of kitchen scraps with a layer of garden waste until the heap is the right height. Cover it all with a thin layer of soil. After three weeks remove the stake. The pile should have subsided by now — add more material if necessary.

Pit composting can be either aerobic or anaerobic. If you completely seal it off with soil it becomes anaerobic, but as long as it can breathe it remains aerobic.

Compost activators

Well-made compost works so fast that activators are not necessary, though some people swear by them. You can buy them or use sprigs of yarrow, soil in which yarrow has been growing, a handful of chamomile flowers or a layer of comfrey leaves. You can also build your heap under the drip line of an elder tree.

Additions to the compost heap

Compost may be acidic. Eggshells or wood ash will help to keep the balance. Rock phosphate may be added but **never add lime.** *If* your garden needs it, give it separately; not in the compost. Dolomite may be used instead.

Anaerobic compost

To make a plastic bag compost, fill one-third of a heavy-duty garbage bag with a mixture of kitchen and garden waste. This is a good way of getting rid of fruit damaged by fruit-fly or codling moths. Seal the bag and leave it out in the sun and weather. Open it every week or so to see how it is doing; if it stinks, and it will as decomposition progresses, it is not ready. When there is no smell you have compost. It can take anything from a fortnight to six weeks to thoroughly decompose.

Kitchen compost

Toss your kitchen scraps into a lidded bucket (nappy buckets are good) and every evening cover them with a layer of sawdust and press down. The sawdust should soak up excess fluid. Keep the bucket covered.

When it is full — and you will be surprised how much goes in as it all compacts — cover it with a layer of sawdust or soil. Up-end the bucket in an out-of-the-way spot in the garden and leave the contents to mature for six weeks to three months, depending on the weather. Compost is made more quickly in summer.

WEED CONTROL

Weeds are opportunists and colonise bare or disturbed soil. The less you disturb the soil by digging, and the more leaf litter and mulch you leave on the ground, the fewer weeds you will have.

In a monoculture, all weeds are unwelcome. In a garden, they can be beneficial. Deep-rooted weeds can bring up leached elements beyond the reach of shallower-rooted plants, and make them available to crops as they decompose. A background weed population provides a year-round 'home-base' for both pests and their predators, so that when pest numbers build up on a planted crop, the predator numbers rise to match them.

In ploughed areas, weeds stabilise soil which might be affected by rain or water run-off. By covering the soil they can help to prevent moisture loss and can tell you a lot about your soil. Sorrel, for instance, grows in acid soil, thistles in soil with a high nitrogen level and bracken in soil with a nitrogen deficiency.

Crops and weeds share the same food resources but it is possible for them to live together without the crop yield being substantially reduced. Once a crop reaches a third of its growth new weeds will not reduce the yield. A steadily growing crop will outgrow weeds.

Weeds can be useful too. Annual weeds that have not seeded can be left to wilt and then used as mulch. Put other weeds in a metal drum, cover them with water and leave for a few weeks. The liquid can be used as manure, the slush as a weed-free mulch.

Establishing a weed-free garden

There are various ways of making sure the soil is as free of weeds as possible before you plant.

1. Sterilise the soil. Do not do this unless you must, as you will kill the good with the bad. Bake a small batch of soil in the oven along with a large potato until the potato is done. 'Cook' a much larger amount in a cut-down 44-gallon drum over an open fire. Build up the fire well and then cover everything with piles of wet newspapers, old hessian, old carpet or whatever you have, and leave for at least half an hour for the soil to get hot.

2. Torch the ground with a flame-gun. This is another 'good-with-the-bad' method.

3. Temporary flooding. Keeping soil under water for three weeks can kill weeds, but may damage the soil.

4. Keep hens, pigs, goats or rabbits on the ground you wish to clear. Hens and rabbits can be kept in open-bottomed cages and moved frequently. The larger animals can be either tethered or contained by a small, round, movable fence made from reinforcing mesh.

5. Dig the ground over, cover it with clear plastic and leave it for three weeks. The heat under the plastic will encourage the weeds to germinate but will kill off their young growth.

6. Dig the ground over, keep well-watered for the next three weeks to encourage any weeds to germinate and then dig them in.

7. Plant a green manure crop. This is done to choke out the weeds. I grow sunflowers from cheap birdseed, slash the tender plants before they flower and leave them on the ground as mulch. Buckwheat is also cheap to buy, grows fast even on poor soil and smothers weeds quickly.

8. Make an above-ground garden bed. Mow or slash the grass and weeds, then cover the whole of the bed with a thick layer of overlapping newspaper. Cover that with a layer, at least one metre deep, of compost, wilted comfrey or lucerne hay and cover that with a thin layer of compost or weed-free soil. Do not use 'first-cut' lucerne as it will have seeds in it. To get rid of weed seeds in the hay, shake it well before using it, or give it to the hens for a while and let them do the job for you. The higher you build the bed the less likely it is that weeds will colonise it.

Controlling weeds

You can remove weeds, kill them or give the crop the strength to outgrow them. Weeds should be dealt with before they can seed. Many weeds — couch grass is a prime example — give off root-toxins which inhibit the growth of nearby plants and so should be removed as soon as detected. Weed control after a third of a crop's life will not help to increase the yield, but if the weeds seed you will have more work later.

Crop rotation can cut down on the build-up of the weeds associated with a particular crop. However, it can also introduce fresh ones when the soil is disturbed. Companion planting can help. Bare ground invites weeds, so plant a low-growing crop with a tall one; for example, sweet potatoes with corn, melons with corn, peas with tall beans or corn. Covering the soil with mulch will smother the weeds but do make sure there are no live weeds in the mulch. Drip irrigation will keep crops growing strongly enough to compete successfully for available food. Minimum tillage will deny the weeds the disturbed ground they need for their seeds to germinate.

If you have an area which defies all your efforts to make it weed-free, dig it all up and plant marigolds, poppies, buckwheat, oats, rye or wheat as thickly as possible so there is no room for the weeds to get in. When the crop is fully grown, slash it, and leave it on the surface as green manure. Use the ground when it is decomposed, or part the residue and plant in the spaces.

Some weeds are more persistent than others:

Bracken

Leaf-drip contains phenolic compounds which suppress the growth of various grains, grasses and trees. It is high in potash, so cut it in spring or summer and either add it to the compost or use it as a mulch. Mow it repeatedly. Bend over any soft new fronds — the bruising weakens them. Keep this up and the bracken will die.

Couch grass

In early spring and onwards, cover it with a thick layer of newspaper, mulch at least 200 mm thick or black plastic. If you leave it till late in the year these methods will not work as well. Even simply covering the couch with a thin layer of mulch makes it easier to pull out. In large areas there is nothing for it but to plough and weed, plough and weed for about two years.

Sorrel

Keep adding organic matter to the soil to reduce the acidity sorrel likes, and to aerate it. Sorrel will disappear as the soil improves.

Oxalis, onion weed, nut grass

Attack them in early spring or late winter when the old bulbs are exhausted and the new ones are about to start growth. Dig over the ground to fork-depth, shake the soil off any bulblets you find and collect them. Keep on digging over, shaking off and collecting until you think that any bulblets left must be too small to survive. You have to be very meticulous and persistent.

Summer grass or crab grass

This is an annual so never let it go to seed. Mow regularly and other grass should choke it out.

Skeleton weed

Slash it before it flowers. If new seedlings keep appearing you will have to keep your eye on it.

Thistles

Mow or behead them just before they flower and rake them up. They are high in silica so use them as compost or as a green manure spray. They like disturbed ground so do not allow stock to overgraze.

Patterson's curse

Never let it flower — one plant can seed four square metres. Mow repeatedly at 'rosette' stage so that the plants lose vigour. In large areas, plough them in or let sheep heavy-graze them.

Blackberries: a lesson in large-scale weed control

Around where I live blackberries grow on abandoned mullock heaps and then make their way to land disturbed for orchards and to pastures that have been overcleared and overgrazed or which 'slump' after heavy rain. The blackberries thrive and put on three metres in height and one metre in width, season after season.

Slowly, though, the picture begins to change. Down in the warm, moist darkness at the centre of the clumps, germination of another type of growth has taken place. *Pittosporum undulatum* is a rainforest fringe tree and it gradually pushes its way to the light through the tangle of blackberry canes. It slowly covers the blackberry clump, which, starved of light and moisture, dwindles and dies. Black wattles can have much the same effect, though they are not as efficient at smothering.

Banana passionfruit, pumpkins and chokos can be grown over the blackberry bushes to weigh them down and starve them of light and air so that their growth becomes stunted, though the bushes may not be killed.

During a drought we slashed down the intrusive blackberry bushes and put stock food on top of them. Wallabies, horses and sheep came for the food, ate the young shoots and trod down what they did not eat. Friends slashed down their bushes and tethered goats to browse on them; when they moved the goats to another bush they sowed grass on the cleared ground — the result, a loam enriched with years of blackberry leaves and recent goat droppings. A neighbour encircled each clump of

19

blackberries with a small electric fence, tossed in a bag of pig nuts and let his pigs go after them. By the time the pigs had finished rooting for the nuts the blackberry bushes were finished too. I built my asparagus bed on a blackberry clump. I trampled it down using boots and a brush hook, threw a thick layer of newspaper over it and covered that with mulch deep enough to plant asparagus in. All I had to do was pull out a few persistent blackberry shoots the following year.

The quickest way to get rid of blackberry bushes is to uproot them and burn them. You will need a bulldozer or a tractor with a front-end loader and the bare soil will have to be replanted at once before weeds take advantage of the disturbed soil. Burning will work if the fire is hot enough. This can mean using a flame gun or pouring diesel oil over the bushes and setting them alight. Again, you will have to replant the disturbed ground at once and in the following season will have to watch for shoots from roots which have escaped the fire.

No one method will work for everyone, but, if you are wholehearted about it, you can manage it.

COMPANION PLANTING

Many plant associations will improve the vigour of your cropping — too many to list here. The following associations are a few that directly involve pest and pathogen control. Some are folklore; some scientifically investigated. Some are successful overseas but may work by attracting predators not known in Australia; others simply change the plant's microclimate, making it less susceptible to stress or disease. All are worth experimenting with.

Any aromatic herbs — especially tansy, lad's love and lavender — help repel insects, especially aphids, by masking the crop. Insect repellent companion crops are most effective if planted at least two weeks before the plants they will protect, or transferred there in a pot.

The more diverse the habitat, the less likely your plant is to be attacked by herbivorous pests — and this diversity includes weed species:

Garlic

Garlic planted under roses is reputed to help the control of black spot. It will also repel borers, mites and weevils around trees and shrubs, especially if the tops are regularly pinched.

Nasturtium, rosemary, coriander, nettle, spearmint and chives.

These are reputed to repel aphids and woolly aphids. Nasturtium flowers repel aphids from crops *above* them, and will also repel whitefly.

Chinese cabbage

Spent Chinese cabbage can be used as a trap for whitefly.

Flowering parsnips

Flowering parsnips help repel codling moth, possibly by attracting predator wasps and hoverflies.

Sage, wormwood, onions, leeks and rosemary

These will repel the carrot fly.

Rue

Rue may deter harlequin beetles from raspberries.

Catnip

This may repel ants.

Celery, hyssop and scented geraniums

These will repel cabbage-white butterfly, as will companion crops of white and red clover, which also add nitrogen to the soil.

Chives

Chives under apples may help prevent apple scab.

Crotaria

Crotaria helps to control eelworms.

Mustard

Mustard controls a range of nematodes.

Yarrow

Yarrow is said to give plants resistance to insect attack.

Corn

Corn planted with sweet potatoes may increase the number of parasitic wasps preying on leaf beetles. When planted with beans, it tends to increase the range of predators for the pests of both plants.

Cotton

Cotton and cowpeas may lead to an increase in parasitic wasps that predate the boll weevil. Cotton or sesame grown with corn reduces the incidence of heliothis caterpillar (corn earworm) by increasing the number of predators.

Strawberries

Strawberries grown under peaches may increase parasites to control oriental fruit moth.

Peanuts

Peanuts grown with corn increases the number of spiders, leading to fewer corn borers.

Blackberries

Blackberries around vineyards appear to reduce the numbers of grape leaf hoppers by increasing alternative hosts for parasitic wasps.

An abundance of various weeds appears to reduce the number of San Jose scale on apple trees, aphids and cabbage-white butterfly caterpillars on brussel sprouts, beanfly on mung beans. Weed cover needs to be manipulated so that it provides diversity without interfering with cropping.

WATERING

Plants are about 80 per cent water; they absorb it through their roots and lose it through their leaves. They wilt when they cannot take in enough to make up their loss and can die from stress or because they cannot absorb sufficient nutrients without enough water.

Sometimes mild water stress can be beneficial. If plants have to send down deeper roots in search of water they 'harden off' — that is, produce less soft, disease prone growth. Fruit trees put out more buds if they are short of water when flower buds are forming, but, once the buds start to develop they stop. Lack of water while the fruit is developing usually keeps it small, but it can have a better flavour, excellent texture and improved keeping quality. Too much water can lead to split fruit.

The aim of every gardener should be to see that the plants have just enough water and not a drop more. These hints will help you achieve this.

Water only when needed

Never water just because it is Tuesday and that's the day you always water; never take the condition of the surface of the soil as the true indication of moisture present. Poke your finger well down into the soil or under the mulch and if it comes out damp, do not water.

Water only the root-depth

There is no point in watering soil that the roots of the plants cannot reach. Shallow-rooted plants like strawberries and lettuce need more frequent but less copious watering than deep-rooted plants like carrots and shrubs. To check on the moisture needed, dig a trench parallel to the row in question and as deep as the roots of the plants. Pour in water and check to see how much is needed for it to penetrate to the bottom of the trench. A bought tensiometer will also tell you when soil needs water.

Increase the humus level of the soil

Humus enables soil to hold water and makes the water readily available to plants.

Mulch the soil

Covering the soil with mulch will prevent the evaporation of moisture and stop the soil from forming a crust which water cannot easily penetrate.

Timing

If you can predict it, water before a hot spell arrives. If you water during the heat of the day, most of the water will be lost to evaporation. Do not water on windy days. Keep overhead watering to a minimum and water in the evenings when the heat of the sun has passed.

If there is any likelihood of downy mildew developing, water in the mornings so that any water on the leaves will be dry by nightfall. Contrary to advice often given, one really good watering a week may not be best for your garden. Plants grow best when the water and food supply is regular and constant. By the end of the week plants could be parched so give as much water as is needed to penetrate the soil to root-depth and water again just before the plant starts to wilt.

Keep plants growing strongly

Healthy plants are better able to take up water and to cope with a lack of it than plants whose growth has been erratic.

Too much water

If the soil is always damp, if moss and algae grow in the grass and if roots and bulbs rot before a plant can flourish, check the amount of water present in the soil. Dig a hole one metre deep; if water begins to seep into it, you have too much water. You will have to divert it and channel it away.

To do this, dig a drain one metre deep on land on the high side of the trouble spot and divert the water away. You may choose to plant water-loving trees, such as willows, casuarinas or melaleucas to absorb as much of the excess water as possible. You can, of course, build above-ground beds and lift them above the water level.

nage caused by the leaf cutter bee

Mealy bug

eping willow rust

Citrus white fly at the immature stage

Typical case moth larvae damage

Evidence of spotting caused by thrips

White wax scale on a citrus stem

A eucalyptus leaf attacked by sawfly

Psyllids

Cottonycushion scale

Juvenile scale

MINERAL DEFICIENCIES IN PLANTS

Mineral deficiencies will be unlikely if you return large quantities of organic matter to the soil. But, if you are just beginning an organic garden or if you live in an area of unusually high rainfall or have problem soil, the following list of symptoms will help you to identify a mineral deficiency. Remember, however, that nitrogen starvation can mimic any of these symptoms. As a first step, use a high-nitrogen food supplement such as blood and bone, hen manure or diluted urine and wait six weeks. If there is still trouble, correct the obvious deficiency.

Boron deficiency

Symptoms: Young leaves are misshapen with yellow margins and brittle stems.
Remedy: Add wood ash, horse manure, compost, sawdust, cow manure or clover clippings to the soil.

Calcium deficiency

Symptoms: Young leaves curl and blacken.
Remedy: Add wood ash, lime or dolomite to acid soils. Alternatively, you can add oat hay, lucerne, good grass hay, blood and bone, sawdust, crushed shells and any manure. Use a foliar spray made from comfrey, chamomile, seaweed or compost water.

Copper deficiency

Symptoms: Veins on the youngest leaves are dark blue and the tips may die. Twisted foliage with sunken spots.
Remedy: Add wood ash, compost, manure or sawdust to the soil. Use a foliar spray of nettle, yarrow, dandelion, chickweed or compost water.

Iron deficiency

Symptoms: Young leaves are pale to white. Most common on wet or alkaline soils or where too much phosphorus has been added.
Remedy: Add manure, compost, wood ash or sawdust to the soil. Use a foliar spray of nettle, seaweed, spinach, silver beet or dandelion.

Magnesium deficiency

Symptoms: Yellow patches on the oldest leaves in particular; the edges remain bright green.
Remedy: Add dolomite or lime to the soil. Use a foliar spray made from green garden matter.

Manganese deficiency

Symptoms: Black spots near the leaf veins, yellow between veins, veins remain light green. Worse in wet weather and on alkaline soil.
Remedy: Add horse manure, wood ash, compost, seaweed, carrot tops, sawdust or lucerne to the soil. Use a foliar spray of compost water, carrot tops, lucerne, chickweed or seaweed.

Molybdenum deficiency

Symptoms: The oldest leaves become yellow and mottled and the edges curl over. The condition is known as "whiptail" in cauliflowers. It is most common on acid soil or soils with a high lead content.

Remedy: Add manure, especially horse manure, wood ash, compost or well-rotted sawdust to the soil. Use a liquid manure spray, or a green manure spray made from green matter grown outside your area.

Nitrogen deficiency

Symptoms: Old leaves become yellow, first of all as new leaves take all the available nitrogen. The plant becomes small and weak. Roses and other flowers may mature early but have a short life with weak stems and petals that drop before the flower opens.

Remedy: Add hen manure, urine, blood and bone, lucerne hay, lawn clippings or chopped legume roots to the soil. They are all rich in nitrogen. Any green foliar spray will help too.

Phosphorus deficiency

Symptoms: Yellowing or purple-tinged leaves, lack of plant vigour.

Remedy: Add phosphorus-rich material such as ground rock phosphate, hen manure, blood and bone, ground bones and eggshells as a short-term measure. Use any green foliar spray.

Potassium deficiency

Symptoms: Foliage blackened round the edges; dark spots surrounded by a pale green ring in the middle of the leaf or along the stem.

Remedy: Add wood ash, seaweed or urine to the soil, or any fresh manure in small doses, but be careful about manure "burn". As a short-term measure use a seaweed foliar spray. All plant residues contain some potash so any organic spray will do.

Sulphur deficiency

Symptoms: Young leaves yellow; purple to dark green veins and downward-pointing edges. The deficiency is common in sandy soils which contain little organic matter.

Remedy: Add green matter to the soil. Use cabbage leaves and garlic, both high in sulphur, to make compost or foliar spray.

Zinc deficiency

Symptoms: Young leaves are small, pale yellow, mottled, narrow and bunched together. Do not confuse this deficiency with nitrogen deficiency in which the oldest, not the youngest leaves are affected.

Remedy: Add wood ash, sawdust, horse manure, compost or ground rock phosphate to the soil. Use liquid manure or a foliar spray made from lucerne, cornstalks or vetch — preferably brought in from another area as they too may be zinc-deficient if grown on the same soil.

Liquid manure

Place a quantity of compost, green matter or animal manure other than dog, pig or human, in a bucket and cover it with water. Put a lid on the bucket and leave it for between a few days and three weeks until the water has become the colour of weak tea. Use the liquid as a foliar spray or to water the ground around the plants. Put the sludge in the compost heap.

The better the materials are, the better the liquid manure will be. Try a mixture of manure, comfrey and pungent herbs. Seaweed liquid manure is reputed to increase plant resistance to pests, diseases and frost.

Garden tonic

Make liquid manure from a mixture of chamomile flowers, comfrey, nettles and seaweed and use as described above as a general fertiliser and tonic. If you do not have all the four ingredients make use of the ones you have.

PESTS AND SEEDLINGS

Ants

Although ants are valuable predators, they cause trouble if they nest under your plants. You can:

1. Use a bait of one part borax to four parts icing sugar and kill the ants.
2. Spray the nest with a mixture of one part kerosene, one part liquid detergent to eight parts of vegetable oil.
3. Pour a bucket of boiling water on the nest and spray the escaping ants with pyrethrum.
4. Grease-band seedlings and shrubs at ground level.

Cutworms

Cutworms chew through the seedling stems just above ground level. You can:

1. Interplant susceptible crops with herbs, onions and marigolds.
2. Mulch the ground with oak leaves.
3. Mulch regularly to help destroy breeding sites and to encourage the presence of a parasitic fungus.
4. Let the soil lie fallow in autumn or spring. It must be completely fallow with no weeds present.
5. **Never** plant seedlings just after a crop of weeds have been dug into the soil.
6. If there are cutworms in the soil, keep it covered with a sheet of clear plastic for three weeks. This should kill the cutworms.

7. Encourage natural cutworm predators: parasitic fungus, flies, wasps, beetles, ibis, starlings, crows, magpies, yellow robins, kookaburras.
8. Before you plant seedlings, spray their roots and the soil with Dipel.
9. Protect seedlings with a "collar" made from either a tin can with top and bottom cut out or the cardboard from a toilet roll. Press the collar into the soil to form a fence around the roots and stem.
10. Dig up an affected seedling at once — you may find the cutworm on the plant. Kill it and replant the seedling.
11. Splint seedlings with two matchsticks.
12. Use a bait: Mix one part bran, one part hardwood sawdust and two parts of molasses with enough water to make the mixture moist. Spread the paste on the soil around the seedlings. It will attract the cutworms and, sticky and helpless, they will be unable to burrow back into the soil and will either die of heat or starvation, or be eaten by birds.

Earwigs

Earwigs like garden debris, wood heaps and slow compost piles, so never plant seedlings near any of them. Trap earwigs by giving them shelters of thin black polythene pipe closed at one end, and flowerpots containing crumpled newspaper. Empty the traps twice a week.

Slugs and snails

Both slugs and snails love to eat tender young seedlings and can do an enormous amount of damage if action is not taken. You can:

1. Use an oak leaf mulch or drizzle the soil with wormwood tea. Seedlings can be sprayed with bordeaux, but too much could induce copper toxicity in the soil.
2. Encourage the natural predators — birds and lizards.
3. Clean up any patches of grass which offer shelter or any plants which overgrow a low stone border or wall.
4. Spread sharp grit, broken shells, dry ash, lime or finely chopped human hair around any area you wish to protect.
5. Salt makes an effective barrier but is toxic in the garden and must be used carefully. Take a length of black polythene pipe 1.25 cm round and make it into a gutter by cutting away the top third of the circumference. Seal off the ends by tying them with wire; fill the gutter with salt and arrange it round the beds like a fence. Snails will not cross it and it is easily moved, but be careful the gutter does not overflow when it rains.
6. Make a fence of tin cans with the top and bottom cut out, standing shoulder to shoulder and press into the soil.
7. Make a metal fence about 40 cm high. The metal should angle outwards and have a downward-pointing edge so that the slugs and snails can shelter under it but not climb over it, and are assembled ready for capture.
8. A small electric fence made with fuse wire, a Big Jim torch battery and icecream sticks really works, so don't laugh. It should stand about 2 mm above the soil.
9. Let hens run in the garden for the last hour before they perch. By then they should have eaten enough green stuff and will only go for delicacies like slugs and snails.
10. Ducks, particularly Khaki Campbells and Indian Runners, can be trained to become slug and snail hunters. Buy them already trained or train them yourself. Do not allow them access to water where they can swim. Give constant access to green stuff and make sure they don't get any other food until after they have had a hard day clearing the slugs and snails.
11. Use traps. Snails are easily trapped but you must be prepared to get rid of bodies every morning. Traps can be made from hollowed-out raw potatoes; squeezed-out orange or grapefruit halves; wilted cabbage leaves smeared with dripping; empty beer cans or cans filled with bran or wheatgerm left in the garden overnight; or an icecream container filled with water, covered with a layer of bran, and sunk into the soil (The bran will entice the pests; the water will drown them.)
12. Snails and slugs will not cross a low, narrow fence of copper. Unfortunately, copper is costly.
13. Make snail soup. Catch snails on a wet night, crush them, put the bodies in a bucket of water, cover it and forget it for a few weeks. The resultant liquid and sludge will be high in nitrogen, calcium and phosphorus and will make a good plant food. It may also be a disease-carrier and act as a deterrent to other snails.

THE VEGETABLE GARDEN

PROBLEMS		
Amaranth	Symptoms:	Plants fall over in wet weather
	Cause:	Mildew
	Solution:	Grow in a sheltered spot with a coarse mulch, such as hay, for support where a well-manured crop has been grown recently. No other feeding is necessary. *Note:* High-nitrogen feeding will cause soft sappy growth prone to mildew and 'lodging'.
Artichokes (globe)	Symptoms:	Chewed leaves
	Cause:	28-spot ladybird
	Solution:	Sprinkle the leaves with derris dust or pyrethrum if you think the depredation is bad enough to stunt the growth of the plant (this is unlikely). *Warning:* Do not confuse the 28-spot ladybird with its relations which have fewer spots — they are valuable predators.
Broad beans	Symptoms:	Brown spots on leaves
	Cause:	Chocolate spot
	Solution:	Add wood ash, compost or comfrey mulch to the soil to supply needed potash; spray leaves with soapy water as soon as the spots appear and repeat every few days; take special care in rainy weather.
	Symptoms:	Shiny black insects clustered on the growing points
	Cause:	Black aphids
	Solution:	Spray the plant with soapy water; put reflective foil on the ground between the rows. You can also nip off the tips and cook them after shaking off the aphids — they are delicious.

PROBLEMS		
Broad beans (continued)	Symptoms: Cause: Solution:	Chewed leaves, empty pods Caterpillars Sprinkle leaves with cayenne pepper; spray plant with Dipel or bug juice; pick pods regularly and encourage birds.
	Symptoms: Cause: Solution:	Velvet-brown pustules on the leaves Rust Do not overhead water; it will spread the spores. Mulch well and dust leaves with powdered sulphur; try a diluted soluble-aspirin spray. If the temperature is under 24ºC, spray with bordeaux.
	Symptoms: Cause: Solution:	Tips become black and die; stems rot from the top downwards and may also rot at ground level Broad bean wilt This is a viral disease carried by aphids and is worse in cold weather. Remove and burn infected plants without delay and get rid of the aphids. Once the temperature rises above 20ºC the plants may recover. Careful tilling of the ground around the plants can help a persistent problem.
Dwarf beans	Symptoms: Solution:	Leaf-curl Don't worry; the leaves curl in cool weather and will straighten out as it gets warmer.
	Symptoms: Cause: Solution:	Brown patches on leaves or beans; rotting stems; beans stuck together Fungus disease Spray every two days with chamomile, chives or milk. If the temperature is under 24ºC, spray with bordeaux or baking soda.
	Symptoms: Cause: Solution:	Dull, rough leaves with webbing on them Red spider mites Spray plants with milk, amise or coriander. Use an all-purpose spray in severe cases.

PROBLEMS		
Dwarf beans (continued)	Symptoms: Solution:	Rotted seed If you plant early when the weather is cold and wet, coat the seeds in salad oil first.
	Symptoms: Cause: Solution:	Plants collapse; brown tunnels form in stems Bean fly Dust with derris every three days. Use a garlic or dilute clay spray. Put boards covered with glue or motor oil around the plants to trap the flies. In badly affected areas grow beans before the weather warms up. Climbing beans are more resistant to bean fly than dwarf beans, and snake beans are relatively untroubled by them. Keep up the phosphorous and potash in the soil — add wood ash or compost. In severe cases use an all-purpose spray.
Beetroot	Symptoms: Cause: Solution:	White, skeletonised leaves Leaf-miner Dust leaves with ground rock sulphate. Use bug juice, garlic or onion spray. *See* **Recipes for pest and disease control**, p.137
	Symptoms: Cause: Solution:	Pale to dark brown spots on the leaves Leaf-spot fungus Do not overhead water; spray with casuarina or chamomile tea; use bordeaux in cool weather.
	Symptoms: Cause: Solution:	Leaves covered with a white powdery film Powdery mildew Pick off affected leaves. Spray with chamomile or chive tea every two days. Dust leaves with powdered sulphur. Spray plant with a solution of Condy's crystals (permanganate of potash). *See* **Recipes for pest and disease control**, p.137.
	Symptoms: Cause: Solution:	Brown sunken patches on the beetroot Boron deficiency Feed the soil around the plants with compost or good-quality mulch. Use a green foliar spray made from material brought in from outside your district.

PROBLEMS		
Brassica (Brussels sprouts, broccoli, cabbage, Chinese cabbage, cauliflower)	Symptoms:	Stunted yellow plants with distorted leaves
	Cause:	Molybdenum deficiency
	Solution:	Soak comfrey or cauliflower leaves from plants grown outside your area until the water turns pale green. Use it as a spray, morning and evening for three weeks, and then reduce to once a week. It is no use attempting to supply molybdenum from compost made from materials in your own district, because they are probably deficient in it too. Cauliflowers are the most susceptible members of the family. Use compost and mulch — an active soil makes elements more available to plants.
	Symptoms:	Brittle areas between the leaf-veins; cabbages are the most obvious sufferers
	Cause:	Magnesium deficiency
	Solution:	Add a teaspoonful of dolomite to soil around the plant and water it in well. If the plants are large, spray the leaves with liquid green manure as well.
	Symptoms:	Pale cabbages that do not last
	Cause:	Phosphorous deficiency
	Solution:	Add ground rock sulphate or old hen manure to the soil.
	Symptoms:	Brittle leaves
	Cause:	Potash deficiency
	Solution:	Sprinkle wood ash on the soil around the plant and water well. A green foliar spray could be a short-term solution.
	Symptoms:	Leaves develop v-shaped brown patches that become thin and brittle; affected seedlings die
	Cause:	Black cabbage rot
	Solution:	A double-strength garlic or chive spray may help, but don't depend on it. Dig out and burn all infected plants once the trouble becomes acute. Leave the ground covered with clear plastic for three weeks after an infection before you consider using it again. Do not invite trouble by planting brassica in the same spot — practise four-year crop rotation.

PROBLEMS

Brassica **(Brussels sprouts,** **broccoli, cabbage,** **Chinese cabbage,** **cauliflower)** (continued)	Symptoms:	Skeletonised foliage; young plants completely eaten away
	Cause:	Cabbage-white butterfly and cabbage moth caterpillars
	Solution:	Surround the beds with strongly perfumed herbs, such as lavender, tansy or rue. Squash every caterpillar you see and leave the body on the plants to attract predators. Interplant brassica with other plants so that the pests find migration from one preferred plant to the next difficult. Dust the plants with powdered rock sulphate and spray with dilute clay, derris or Dipel, bug juice, pepper, garlic, quassia or wormwood. Make a number of tiny three-sided boxes no more than 10 mm high, scatter some lime or wood ash inside and place them strategically around the plants you wish to protect. The caterpillars may shelter in them and become dehydrated on the lime.
	Symptoms:	Cauliflowers with purple or yellow heads
	Solution:	Curl the leaves over the heads to protect them while they mature. Direct sunlight will not do any good, but discoloured heads will do you no harm either.
	Symptoms:	Loose broccoli heads
	Solution:	Pick them earlier.
	Symptoms:	Knobbly roots; plants that grow too slowly, wilt, especially in hot weather and die easily
	Cause:	Club root caused by nematodes
	Solution:	Grow a companion crop of marigolds which inhibit some nematodes. Keep up the organic content of the soil, particularly if it is sandy. Add a sprinkle of lime or dolomite if it is too acid. Use tin cans with the top and bottom cut out as protective 'armour' for the plants. Sink them into the soil around each plant. Once you have nematode trouble, do not grow any member of the brassica family, or swedes or turnips, in the trouble spot for at least four years.

PROBLEMS		
Brassica (Brussels sprouts, broccoli, cabbage, Chinese cabbage, cauliflower) (continued)	Symptoms: Cause: Solution:	Small insects on wilted or deformed leaves Aphids Wait at least three weeks for predators to arrive before resorting to using a spray. Try and blast the pests off the leaves with strong jets of water. Plant marigolds or nasturtiums as a companion crop. Place reflective foil between plants. If you must, use a dilute clay, seaweed or nettle spray; a washing soda and soap spray in cool weather is also effective. If nothing works, then bring out derris, lantana, rhubarb, onion and elder sprays.
	Symptoms: Cause: Solution:	Chewed leaves Slugs and snails See **Slugs and snails**, p.28.
	Symptoms: Cause: Solution:	Chewed leaves Caterpillars Dust leaves with cayenne pepper. Use dilute clay spray then Dipel or derris if the pepper doesn't work. Squash the caterpillars and wait for predators.
Chinese cabbage	Symptoms: Cause: Solution:	Cabbages run to seed without hearting Planting at the wrong time Always plant in late autumn or early spring so that the plant matures before the weather warms up. Mulch well to keep soil cool.
Capsicum	Symptoms: Cause: Solution:	Brown spots on fruit and leaves Fungus spot Do not overhead water. Spray with casuarina or horsetail tea. *See* **Recipes for pest and disease control**, p.137
	Symptoms: Cause: Solution:	Small white maggots in fruit. Fruit-fly See **Fruit-fly**, pp.87-88

PROBLEMS

Carrots	Symptoms:	Poor germination
	Solution:	Add humus to the soil and do not allow a crust to form on top. Sow radish and carrot seed together so that radish seed, which germinates quickly, will break up the soil and make it easy for the carrot stem to push its way upward. Keep the ground covered with a thin layer of lawn clippings or sawdust or piece of hessian until the seedlings break through the soil.
	Symptoms:	Cracked carrots
	Cause:	Too much rain or erratic watering
	Solution:	Plant in a well-drained soil and mulch well so that the soil does not dry out. Without regular watering you must expect your carrots to crack.
	Symptoms:	Rotted carrots
	Cause:	Too much moisture; injury to plants
	Solution:	Improve the drainage or raise the growing bed. In wet conditions carrots grown by the no-dig method do better than those in deeply dug soil. Do not dig around maturing carrots.
	Symptoms:	Deformed lumpy carrots with small swellings
	Cause:	Nematodes — root eelworm
	Solution:	Plant a companion crop of marigolds or mustard to drive the eelworm away. Compost will inhibit them too, so keep up the levels in the soil. Soak the ground with a solution of one part molasses to ten parts water — this may dehydrate them. If the infestation is bad you must dig everything out and leave the ground fallow for a month — no growth of any sort must be allowed, not even weeds. The only way to prevent further infestation is to practise rigorous crop rotation.
	Symptoms:	Small green insects in the leaves
	Cause:	Carrot aphid
	Solution:	Hose the leaves vigorously, especially on the underside, and blast the pests off.

THE ORGANIC GARDEN DOCTOR

PROBLEMS

Carrots (continued)	Symptoms:	Holes eaten into the carrots
	Cause:	Carrot-fly larvae
	Solution:	Do not sow the seed in straight rows; sow in blocks. Sow carrot and spring onion seed together. Keep a permanent border of spring onions around the carrot bed.
	Symptoms:	Carrots are a soft, smelly mess
	Cause:	Clumsy post-harvest handling; clumsy pre-harvest digging or weeding
	Solution:	Do not attempt to store any carrot which shows sign of damage. Never store in plastic bags. Use paper or netting and ensure there is plenty of ventilation in the storage space. Make certain the carrots have been thoroughly dried in the sun before even thinking of storing them. Do not dig round the growing carrots; smother any weeds with mulch. If you haven't any, water the ground well so that the weeds are easy to pull out by hand. Do not grow carrots in ground where rot has been a problem for at least another three years.
	Symptoms:	Forked carrots
	Solution:	Make certain there are no stones in the soil; forking is usually caused by the growing root meeting an obstruction. Improve the food supply to the carrots; add compost or good mulch to the soil.
Celery	Symptoms:	Small tough sticks
	Cause:	Insufficient feeding
	Solution:	Give a weekly dose of liquid manure. Keep plants well watered.
	Symptoms:	Seedlings die off quickly; a brown ring forms through the stem of the plant at ground level
	Cause:	Damping off
	Solution:	Plant in partial shade. Try stringing up hessian to give them shelter. Dip each seedling in chamomile tea before putting it in the soil. Pour the surplus tea around the young plants.

PROBLEMS

Celery (continued)	Symptoms: Cause: Solution:	Chewed leaves Slugs and snails See **Slugs and snails**, p.28.
	Symptoms: Cause: Solution:	Small insects clustered on leaves Aphids Squash the pests and leave the bodies on the plants for the predators to clean up. Spray the plants with seaweed, nettle, lantana or onion and if none of these is effective use garlic or pyrethrum. Marigolds planted nearby and reflective foil put down on the soil between the rows both help to deter aphids.
	Symptoms: Cause: Solution:	Dark spots on the leaves which have curled up edges Celery leaf spot Spray plants with chamomile tea every two days or with bordeaux every two weeks. Wash the celery well before eating it.
Chicory	Symptoms: Solution:	Bitter taste Keep plants fed and well watered. Mulch heavily. Place a plant-pot or fruit box over them three days before picking to blanch them.
Choko	Symptoms: Solution:	Roots rot Only plant choko in well-drained soil. Mulch well. Roots may rot if winter is cold.
Cucumbers	Symptoms: Cause: Solution:	Deformed, lumpy roots Eelworms (nematodes) Put a tin can with the top and bottom cut out over each seedling and sink the edges down into the soil to form a barrier against the eelworms. Deter the pests by adding humus to the soil and mulching well and also by planting a companion crop of marigolds.

PROBLEMS

Cucumbers (continued)	Symptoms: Cause: Solution:	Misshapen fruit Poor pollination Grow lemon balm and flowers nearby so that bees are attracted to the area. Do not use sprays which would kill bees.
	Symptoms: Cause:	Grey film on the leaves Powdery mildew
	Symptoms: Cause: Solution:	Leaves shrivel; white clumps of fungus on the undersides Downy mildew *Note:* Both problems have the same remedy. Do not overhead water. Water soil around plants carefully or use drip-irrigation. Mulch soil around plants to prevent any spores splashing up on to foliage during watering. Use seaweed spray to help the plant build up a resistance to mildew. As soon as symptoms appear, spray with milk, chamomile, chive or casuarina every few days. Dust leaves with powdered sulphur. As a last resort spray with half-strength bordeaux, baking soda or Condy's crystals at night, making sure the spray does not touch the blossoms. See **Recipes for pest and disease control**, p.137
	Symptoms: Solution:	Bitter fruit Pick when still green; do not wait until the skins turn yellow. A spell of cool weather can cause the fruit to become bitter.
	Symptoms: Cause: Solution:	Clusters of tiny insects on the underside of stunted, curled leaves Melon aphids which suck the leaf sap; the females fly from plant to plant and populations build up rapidly in hot weather. Hose the underside of the leaves to dislodge the pests, or wipe off with a soapy kitchen cloth. Spray with nettle or wormwood and wait for lacewings and ladybirds to arrive and eat the pests.

PROBLEMS

Cucumbers (continued)	Symptoms: Cause: Solution:	Dull, rough foliage; skeletonised leaves Red spider mite Watering thoroughly may be sufficient; otherwise use anise or coriander spray. An all-purpose spray may be used in bad cases.
Eggplant (Aubergine)	Symptoms: Cause: Solution:	Blistered patch on fruit Sun-scorch Grow plants in a clump or in the shelter of tall plants such as corn or trellised cucumbers.
	Symptoms: Cause: Solution:	Stunted deformed leaves Aphids Grow with wormwood, tansy, marigolds or lavender. Spray with dilute Vegemite to help attract predators like lacewings and hover-flies. Encourage birds and ladybirds. Plant plenty of flowering shrubs and do not use pesticides — even organic ones — unless absolutely necessary. Wait at least three weeks for predators to build up before using either a dilute clay, nettle, wormwood, rhubarb or seaweed spray. As a last resort try derris, wormwood, rhubarb leaf or garlic sprays. In cold weather try a baking soda and soap spray. If you are really pestered with aphids use reflective foil between plants.
	Symptoms: Cause: Solution:	Powdery film on leaves Mildew Do not overhead water in humid areas; mulch the plants well. Pick off affected leaves and spray with chamomile tea every two days. Use seaweed spray as a preventative in hot weather. Spray affected leaves with horsetail or casuarina; use half strength bordeaux or baking powder spray as a last resort.
Endive	Symptoms: Cause: Solution:	Chewed leaves Slugs and snails See **Slugs and snails**, p.28.

PROBLEMS		
Garlic	Symptoms: Cause: Solution:	Powdery film on leaves Mildew Spray with chamomile or chive tea. Use bordeaux in cold weather.
	Symptoms: Cause: Solution:	Leaves wilt and shrivel Root-rot Always make sure soil is well drained and the organic matter in it is decomposed before you plant in it.
	Symptoms: Cause: Solution:	Stems rot at ground level Collar-rot Keep fresh organic matter away from the stems in damp or humid weather.
Leeks	Symptoms: Cause: Solution:	Shrivelled leaf tips Downy mildew Cut off affected tips and mulch the soil around the plants to keep them growing strongly. Do not overhead water. Spray with casuarina tea. Try milk or lilac spray.
Lettuce	Symptoms: Solution:	Bitter taste Transplant seedlings during a cold spell and keep soil moist. Do not allow any check in growth; keep plants well fed and watered until ready to pick.
	Symptoms: Solution:	Premature bolting Cut off two-thirds of the top before you plant seedlings so as to cut down on water loss in the early stages. If the weather is hot, keep a sprinkler on the young plants for their first few days in the soil. Mulch well to avoid fluctuation in soil temperature. Plant bolt-resistant varieties such as Narromar, Red Mignonette and Great Lakes.
	Symptoms: Cause: Solution:	Chewed leaves Slugs and snails See **Slugs and snails**, p.28.

PROBLEMS

Lettuce (continued)	Symptoms:	Slimy leaves
	Cause:	Too much overhead watering or too much rain and humidity
	Solution:	Put plenty of mulch around plants to keep soil moist and prevent contact between plant and soil.
	Symptoms:	Lettuce without a heart
	Cause:	Too much water and nitrogen fed to the plant
	Solution:	Mulch with a low-nitrogen mulch such as paper.
	Symptoms:	Big veins
	Cause:	Viral disease
	Solution:	Dig out plants and burn them. Do not replant lettuce in the same spot for several years. If collecting your own seed, take it only from healthy plants.
	Symptoms:	Small green insects clustered on leaves
	Cause:	Aphids
	Solution:	Grow near wormwood, tansy or marigolds. Use wormwood, nettle, rhubarb or garlic spray. Place reflective foil between plants.
	Symptoms:	Pale to dark brown spots on leaves
	Cause:	Downy mildew
	Solution:	Do not overhead water; mulch the plants well. Use seaweed spray as a preventative and milk, chive or chamomile spray as a control.
Marrow *See* Zucchini		
Melons	Symptoms:	Grey film on leaves
	Cause:	Powdery mildew
	Solution:	See downy mildew, next page.

PROBLEMS		
Melons (continued)	Symptoms:	Shrivelled leaves with yellow blotches on the top and tufts of white fungus on the underside
	Cause:	Downy mildew
	Solution:	*Note:* Both problems have the same remedy. Grow melons on a thick straw mat, on a pile of mown grass or in a spadeful of compost. You can also grow them on stakes. Do not overhead water. Once they are established allow chickens, wombats, wallabies, rabbits or sheep to graze the surrounds to keep the grass down. Use seaweed spray as a preventative. Spray infected leaves with milk, chamomile, lilac, chives or casuarina or dust them with powdered sulphur. As a last resort use double strength garlic spray.
Mushrooms	Symptoms:	Maggots in mushrooms, tiny flies hovering around
	Cause:	Mushroom fly
	Solution:	Pick out affected caps and stalks each day. Spray with pyrethrum.
Okra	Symptoms:	Woodiness
	Cause:	Picked too late
	Solution:	Pick more often.
	Symptoms:	Poor germination
	Solution:	Soak seed in warm water for 24 hours before planting 1 cm deep. Expect germination in about two weeks.
	Symptoms:	Chewed leaves
	Cause:	Caterpillars
	Solution:	Pick off caterpillars by hand. Sprinkle ground rock phosphate on the leaves. Use sprays of dilute clay, derris or Dipel. *See* **Recipes for pest and disease control**, p.137
	Symptoms:	Plant wilts; base of stem rots
	Cause:	Fusarium and venticillium wilt
	Solution:	*See* **Tomatoes.**

PROBLEMS		
Onions	Symptoms:	Distorted leaves with white flecks
	Cause:	Thrips
	Solution:	Dislodge pests by strong jets of water. Spray with soapy water in cool weather. Use a spray of onion, derris, pyrethrum or bug juice. *See* **Recipes for pest and disease control**, p.137
	Symptoms:	Shrivelled tops
	Cause:	Downy mildew
	Solution:	Spray with chive or chamomile tea every three days. You can try lilac spray too. Spray with double strength garlic every 10 days. Spray with bordeaux every two weeks.
	Symptoms:	Plant rots at neck of stem
	Cause:	Wounds from spade or fork
	Solution:	Mulch the ground around onions instead of cultivating it with a spade or fork. Make sure the onion tops have completely withered before cutting them off. Do not use high-nitrogen fertilisers. Spraying with bordeaux will toughen the skins and make them less susceptible to rot.
	Symptoms:	Rotten onions covered in white fungus
	Cause:	White rot
	Solution:	Improve drainage and make sure no undecomposed organic matter is dug into the soil — keep it on top of the soil as mulch.
	Symptoms:	Hollowed out stems
	Cause:	Stems eaten by the larvae of 7 mm maggots of brown hairy flies
	Solution:	Build up sandy soil with mulch but do not dig undecomposed organic matter into the soil. Make a barrier of aromatic herbs or wood ash between the plants to deter the flies.
Parsnips	Symptoms	Small green insects on leaves
	Cause:	Carrot aphid
	Solution::	Spray with garlic. Interplant with onions.

PROBLEMS		
Parsnips (continued)	Symptoms:	Black root tops. Wilted parsnips. Brown-spotted leaves
	Cause:	Canker
	Solution:	Improve drainage. Make sure all organic matter in the soil is decomposed before seed is sown. Do not dig in any more organic matter — leave it to decompose naturally on top of the soil.
	Symptoms:	Poor germination
	Cause:	Elderly seed
	Solution:	Parsnip seed is only viable for a year. Soak bought seed overnight and cover it with sacking until you can see if it is going to germinate. Once parsnips are growing in the garden, allow them to seed themselves naturally.
	Symptoms:	Grey film on foliage
	Cause:	Powdery mildew
	Solution:	Do not overhead water. Cut off all infected foliage. Spray with chamomile, casuarina or double-strength garlic. Use bordeaux or baking soda spray in bad cases. Dust leaves with powdered sulphur. *See* **Recipes for pest and disease control, p.137**
Peas	Symptoms:	Grey film on leaves
	Cause:	Powdery mildew
	Solution:	Stake the peas so that air can flow round them. To maximise the area exposed to the wind, angle the rows so that wind flows down them not across them. Use seaweed spray as a preventative in humid areas and milk, chamomile, garlic or casuarina spray when foliage is affected. In bad cases use bordeaux or baking soda spray. *See* **Recipes for pest and disease control, p.137**
	Symptoms:	Dark spots on leaves
	Solution:	Treat as for powdery mildew above.
	Symptoms:	Empty pods
	Solution:	Wait for warmer weather. Protect against possible predation by birds.

PROBLEMS

Peas (continued)	Symptoms:	Dark brown edges or splodges on leaves; stem may also be affected; both leaves and stem may shrivel
	Cause:	Bacterial blight
	Solution:	Dig out and burn all infected plants. Treat remaining plants as for powdery mildew. Do not pick or weed peas in wet weather. Do not plant the same area with peas for at least three years.
Potatoes	Symptoms:	Dark spots and green-white mould spreading over the leaves which die; lesions appear on stems; rotting tubers
	Cause:	Potato blight; the fungus spores are washed down on to the soil from the leaves and the potatoes rot; the blight is carried by wind, water and infected plants.
	Solution:	Spray with bordeaux as soon as symptoms appear. Spray again after two weeks if symptoms continue. If they are still present near harvest time, slash off the potato tops and burn them, then spray the stalks with bordeaux. The crop will be reduced but there will be less risk of losing it all.
	Symptoms:	Rotting potatoes
	Cause:	The larvae of the potato moth
	Solution:	Hill soil round the plants and add mulch so that the potatoes are not exposed to the female moth which will burrow into them to lay her eggs.
	Symptoms:	Small spots on the leaves which eventually die off — this happens so slowly it looks as though the plant is dying off naturally; reduced yield
	Cause:	Target spot
	Solution:	Spray with bordeaux as soon as symptoms appear and every two weeks thereafter.
	Symptoms:	Green potatoes
	Cause:	Potatoes left on the surface of the ground and exposed to sunlight become bitter and poisonous, due to solanine, an alkaloidal glucocide.
	Solution:	Bag newly dug potatoes at once and store in a dark place.

PROBLEMS		
Potatoes (continued)	Symptoms:	Soggy potatoes
	Solution:	Add wood ash to the soil to supply needed potash. Mulch with comfrey or good compost, but not too much or the soil may become too alkaline.

Warning: **Do not eat green potatoes.**

	Symptoms:	Small insects clustered on stems and leaves; plants may wilt and die
	Cause:	Aphids
	Solution:	Blast pests off plants with strong jets of water. Spray with dilute clay, lantana, onion, garlic, elder, nettle or wormwood. Put down reflective foil between the rows.
	Symptoms:	Wart-like swelling on the tuber skins
	Cause:	Eelworm
	Solution:	Eelworm eggs and larvae can survive in the soil for two years so mulch infected ground well to encourage earthworms which eat them, and fungi which trap them in mycellium webs. Plant an eelworm-resistant crop of rye, wheat or oats nearby and use it as green manure or use the ground for sweetcorn, onions, cauliflowers or cabbage, all of which are eelworm-resistant.
	Symptoms:	Small brown circular or oval encrustations on the skin of the tuber; the leaves look quite healthy
	Cause:	Potato scab
	Solution:	Only plant tubers which have no scabs on the skin. Make sure drainage is good. Spores can remain active in the soil for 15 years or more. Wet soils below 18°C are particularly susceptible.
	Symptoms:	Leaves develop rolled edges, yellow veins and mottled spots
	Cause:	Viral disease carried by aphids
	Solution:	Dig out infected crop and get rid of aphids. The virus will not remain in the soil once the tubers and aphids have gone and a new crop can be planted in the same spot once you are sure all small potatoes have been removed. Do not use small tubers with long thin shoots as seed potatoes; they may be infected with leaf-roll.

PROBLEMS

Potatoes (continued)	Symptoms:	There are no symptoms above ground but scabs will gradually cover the underground tuber
	Cause:	Common scab
	Solution:	Only plant certified seed. Do not grow in ground where beetroot or turnips have been growing. Do not use lime on the potato bed. Mulch well to keep the ground moist, particularly when the tubers are forming and particularly if the conditions are warm and dry and the soil light and sandy. Once scab is a problem, green manure the ground before planting potatoes and make sure it contains plenty of compost and decomposing organic matter which encourage soil micro-organisms antagonistic to scab.
	Symptoms:	New shoots rot; leaves are bunched and curled; tubers are cracked and have brownish-black scabby lumps on them
	Cause:	*Rhizoctonia* scab
	Solution:	Only use blemish-free tubers as seed. Make sure soil is well mulched and drained.
	Symptoms:	Rotten, foul-smelling potatoes
	Cause:	Potato gangrene
	Solution:	Do not damage the tubers when weeding or digging — gangrene only affects injured plants. Do not store damaged potatoes, as even a small wound can let fungus spores enter and one bad potato can infect others. Clear all dirt and debris from past crops from storage area.
	Symptoms:	Caterpillars in the rolled edges of leaves
	Cause:	Potato moth
	Solution:	Encourage bird and wasp predators; use dilute clay spray or Dipel. If problem becomes severe, use a garlic or pyrethrum spray.
Pumpkins	Symptoms:	Aphids clustered on stems and leaves
	Solution:	Squash any on new shoots between your fingers. Pumpkins usually grow so strongly that aphids on them do not matter.

PROBLEMS		
Pumpkins (continued)	Symptoms:	Grey film on the leaves; leaves have a tuft of white fungus on the underside; they shrivel.
	Cause:	Powdery mildew and downy mildew
	Solution:	Prune off affected leaves as soon as they appear. Spray with milk, chamomile, lilac, elder or double strength garlic. Powdery mildew can also be treated with Condy's crystal. *See* **Recipes for pest and disease control**, p.137 Limit overhead watering and water only in the morning so that leaves will not stay wet overnight. Stake the vine to allow air to circulate round the leaves. Grow on top of mulch and do not allow pumpkin to touch the soil. If the weather is cool use a bordeaux or baking soda spray but do not let it touch flowers or new leaves.
Radish	Symptoms:	Cracked radish
	Solution:	Mulch well. Keep water supply steady. Do not allow soil to be too wet and then too dry.
	Symptoms:	Hot taste
	Cause:	Age
	Solution:	Pick radish when young
Rhubarb	Symptoms:	Too many leaves
	Cause:	Too much nitrogen at the expense of other nutrients in the food supply.
	Solution:	A good quality mulch or compost is the only food rhubarb needs.
	Symptoms:	Crown rots; young leaves shrivel
	Cause:	Bacterial crown rot
	Solution:	Dig out and burn infected plants. Spray the remainder with bordeaux in winter and chamomile or elder in summer. Leave the holes in the soil open to the weather for three weeks.
	Symptoms:	Shrivelled leaves with tufts of fungus on the underside
	Cause:	Downy mildew

PROBLEMS		
Rhubarb (continued)	Symptoms:	Brownish spots on the leaves
	Cause:	Leaf spot fungus
	Symptoms:	Yellowish-brown circles on leaves
	Cause:	Rust
	Solution:	All problems have the same remedy. Do not overwater. Make sure soil is well drained. Do not overfertilise, especially in winter. Spray with bordeaux or baking soda in winter and milk, chamomile or elder in summer. *See* **Recipes for pest and disease control**, p.137. If rhubarb grows well but remains green, you have a green variety.
Shallots	Symptoms:	Rotted bulbs and shrivelled leaves with tufts of white fungus on the underside
	Cause:	White rot and downy mildew
	Solution:	Cut out affected plants and spray the remainder with chamomile, elder or double strength garlic in warm weather and baking soda spray in winter. Keep soil well drained; raise the bed if necessary. Make sure all organic matter in the soil is well rotted.
Silver beet	Symptoms:	Pale, stunted plants
	Cause:	Underfeeding
	Solution:	Feed with blood and bone, liquid manure, old hen manure, good mulch or diluted urine — all high in nitrogen.
	Symptoms:	Brown spots on leaves
	Cause:	Fungus leaf spot
	Solution:	Pick off affected leaves. Keep plant growing strongly. Mulch well. Spray with chamomile tea once a week; if this fails use elder or double strength garlic spray, or spray with bordeaux or baking soda in the cool of the evening.
Spinach	Symptoms:	Premature bolting
	Solution:	Grow spinach only in cool weather. Mulch well. Plant the bolt-resistant varieties, Slow Bolt and Summertime.

PROBLEMS		
Squash		*See* Pumpkin, Zucchini
Sunflowers	Symptoms:	General decline, root-rot, spotted leaves
	Cause:	Parsnip canker
	Solution:	Dig out and burn infected plants. Improve soil drainage and do not plant sunflowers or parsnips in the infected soil for at least three years.
Swedes	Symptoms:	Small clusters of insects on foliage
	Cause:	Aphids
	Solution:	Spray plants with soapy water or dilute clay. If this fails to clear the pests, use garlic or pyrethrum in warm weather and washing soda spray in winter. Grow swedes in ground that has been well manured for a previous crop and do not use any high-nitrogen fertiliser subsequently.
	Symptoms: Solution:	Caterpillars chewing the leaves Pick off by hand; encourage birds to come and eat the pests. Spray plants with dilute clay or white pepper. *See* **Recipes for pest and disease control.** Try Dipel if you must.
	Symptoms:	Plants die because the roots rot
	Solution:	Only plant swedes in well-drained soil in which all organic matter is thoroughly decomposed.
Sweet corn	Symptoms:	Poor germination
	Solution:	Do not plant in rows; plant in blocks at least a metre wide.
	Symptoms:	Chewed-out kernels
	Cause:	Corn ear worms which burrow into the kernels and are protected from predators, dusts and sprays by the tough covering of the ear
	Solution:	Part the silk, look for droppings and sawdust-like deposits, track down the worm and squash it — or them. You could inject oil behind the silk but squashing is more effective. Wiping the silk with mineral oil once a week will act as a deterrent; encouraging birds to visit the garden is the best preventative.

PROBLEMS

Sweet corn (continued)	Symptoms:	Young plants die; stems are cut through at ground level
	Cause:	Eelworms, cutworms
	Solution:	Before sowing a large crop of corn in a sandy area, grow, and dig in, a green manure crop of mustard. It will take only between six and eight weeks. For smaller plantings keep up the level of organic matter in the soil. Using toothpicks as miniature stakes, support each seedling so the worms can't get at them; dribble a molasses solution on the soil around each plant. *See* **Recipes for pest and disease control,** p.137
Sweet potatoes	Symptoms:	Large areas of eaten foliage
	Cause:	Cutworms
	Solution:	Drizzle a solution of one part molasses to twenty of water on soil around each plant. Stake plants and lift them above the soil. Keep up organic matter in the soil, particularly in sandy areas. Grow marigolds nearby as a deterrent to the cutworms. *See* **Pests and seedlings,** p.27.
Tomatoes	Symptoms:	Maggots in the fruit
	Cause:	Fruit-fly
	Solution:	Use traps and repellents. Pick fruit regularly. Do not let fallen fruit lie on the ground. *See* **Fruit-fly,** pp.87-88
	Symptoms:	Chewed leaves
	Cause:	Caterpillars of the cabbage-white butterfly
	Solution:	Use dilute clay, white pepper or garlic spray. *See* **Recipes for pest and disease control,** p.137. Try Dipel.
	Symptoms:	Chewed leaves, slimy trails
	Cause:	Slugs and snails
	Solution:	*See* **Slugs and snails,** p.28.
	Symptoms:	Dark patch on the fruit
	Cause:	Blossom-end rot
	Solution:	Water regularly and supply calcium through a green foliar spray of comfrey, chamomile or seaweed. Half strength bordeaux can also be sprayed on the plants. Mulch well to reduce water stress.

PROBLEMS		
Tomatoes (continued)	Symptoms: Solution:	Cracked tomatoes Keep the water supply steady; do not let soil dry out between waterings. Mulch soil well and keep it well drained.
	Symptoms: Cause: Solution:	Plant stems are cut off at ground level Cutworms Make collars of tin cans with top and bottom cut out, or place the stiff cardboard centres of toilet-rolls around each seedling. Alternatively, support the seedlings with two toothpicks used as stakes. The best preventative is either to dig in a green manure crop of mustard before planting, or to make sure you plant only in a well-mulched soil.
	Symptoms: Solution:	Seedlings 'damp-off', they collapse suddenly; stem rots at ground level Make sure all organic matter in the soil is decomposed and that no mulch is touching the seedlings. Before planting any more, dip each seedling in chamomile tea and pour some tea around each one as it is planted.
	Symptoms: Cause: Solution:	Hard yellow patches on ripe, or near-ripe, tomatoes Shortage of phosphorus and potash Spray leaves with compost, seaweed, hen manure, comfrey or urine. *See* **Recipes for pest and disease control, p.137**
	Symptoms: Cause: Solution:	Plant wilts; rots at the base, stem may crack; in mild cases the plant may just grow slowly and look pale and stunted. Fusarium wilt Spray plant thoroughly with double strength garlic as soon as symptoms appear. In bad cases dig out all affected plants and burn them, then cover the holes left with clear plastic after drenching them with double strength garlic spray. It will take at least three weeks to kill the spores in the soil. In future keep the soil high in potash by adding some wood ash or compost; plant fusarium wilt-resistant cultivars; practise crop rotation.

PROBLEMS		
Tomatoes (continued)	Symptoms: Cause: Solution:	Webbed leaves Red spider mites Spray tops and undersides with white oil if the temperature is less than 24°C, or with soapy water in the evening. Otherwise use derris, pyrethrum or nicotine spray.
	Symptoms: Solution:	Poor fruit set If foliage is thick and green the plant has probably been fed too much nitrogen. Add compost and mulch to the soil. *See* **Enriching the soil**, p.13. Add some ground rock phosphate to the soil as a temporary measure.
Turnips	Symptoms: Solution:	Aphids on the leaves Must keep the plants growing strongly.
	Symptoms: Solution:	Caterpillars on the leaves Spray with white pepper or dilute clay. *See* **Recipes for pest and disease control**, p.137. Use Dipel only if you must. Strongly growing turnips will withstand the depredation of aphids.
Zucchini	Symptoms: Cause: Solution:	Woodiness Age Pick them when young.
	Symptoms: Solution:	Grey film on leaves Do not try to grow them in hot humid weather. Keep leaves dry by watering around the base of the plant early in the morning. Mulch well to stop spores splashing up from the soil and on to the plants. Pick off and burn all affected leaves as soon as they appear. Spray with elder or chamomile at any time; with soapy spray in the cool of the evening and with bordeaux or Condy's crystals when temperature is below 24°C. *See* **Recipes for pest and disease control**, p.137. If you have had problems with mildew in a previous season, plant a second crop of zucchini as far away from the first one as possible and in a well-drained airy spot. This way you will make sure of having *some* zucchini.

FRUIT

PROBLEMS		
Apples	Symptoms:	Sunken circular areas of flesh, soft and granular underneath the skin. Flesh breaks down during storage
	Cause:	Bitter pit
	Solution:	Add dolomite to the soil as a long-term solution. It may take two seasons to work. The trouble is caused because the tree has not taken up enough calcium as it matured. This could be due to heavy pruning, not enough moisture or too much nitrogenous food. Put some wood ash and seaweed mulch around the tree and spray the leaves with compost or comfrey every second morning for two weeks.
	Symptoms:	Fruit becomes deformed and develops dark brown, corky patches
	Cause:	Scab
	Solution:	Spray with bordeaux or full-strength urine when trees are dormant. Spray again at bud-swell if the problem is severe. When the tree is in leaf, spray with a solution of one in 10 urine to prevent the scab spreading. Add potash to the soil.
	Symptoms:	Greyish powdery film on leaves and buds; fruit is covered with a fine 'tracery'. Jonathon apples are particularly susceptible.
	Cause:	Powdery mildew
	Solution:	Cut out withered shoots in winter and spray with bordeaux, baking soda or a solution of Condy's crystals when the tree is dormant. Urine spray may help. Add potash to the soil.
	Symptoms:	Rotting wood
	Cause:	Collar-rot and other wood rots
	Solution:	Cut away as much affected wood as possible and paint the wounds with bordeaux paste. *See* **Recipes for pest and disease control**, p.137. Dig away the soil from as many affected roots as possible and leave them exposed to the air.

PROBLEMS

Apples (continued)	Symptoms:	Dark, blackish, splitting bark and dead wood
	Cause:	Canker
	Solution:	Paint pruning wounds or any visible injury with bordeaux paste. Spray with bordeaux before pruning. A winter spray of bordeaux will kill any canker spores on the tree.
	Symptoms:	Small hole in side of fruit; tunnel from calyx end of fruit to the seed; flesh brown and eaten
	Cause:	Codling moth
	Solution:	*See* **Codling moth**, pp.88-90
	Symptoms:	Sticky, white woolly ovals on stems and leaves
	Cause:	Woolly aphids
	Solution:	Wait for natural predators. If they do not rescue you in time, pick the pests off by hand or dab them with methylated spirits. Use a dilute clay, coriander or anise spray, or, if you must, a derris, rhubarb leaf, coriander, garlic or elder spray.
	Symptoms:	Chewed leaves, tunnels in fruit
	Cause:	Light brown apple moth
	Solution:	This native moth has many predators, so do not use sprays to kill them. From around the trees, remove weeds that allow them over-wintering sites. Allow chickens or sheep to close-graze around the trees when they are dormant. Encourage birds, spiders and wasps to visit the orchard. Use Dipel.
	Symptoms:	Distorted leaves or flowers; premature petal drop; small, black droppings on stems and leaves
	Cause:	Thrips
	Solution:	Rain or hot dry weather, wasps, ladybirds and lacewings will usually take care of the problem. If they do not, jet the pests off the bushes with hot water or use as a dilute clay or soapy water spray, and onion or derris as a last resort. If thrips have been persistent during the growing season, use an oil and pyrethrum spray in winter. Some thrips predate mites and aphids, so do not go in for wholesale slaughter.

PROBLEMS

Apples (continued)	Symptoms:	'Sand-blasted' looking leaves, usually worse near the bottom of the tree
	Cause:	Red spider mite
	Solution:	Slash weeds around the affected tree or mulch over them. Overhead water when the weather is hot and dry. Spray with milk, coriander or anise. Onion and garlic sprays are effective but will kill beneficial predators too. Try an oil spray — but only in cool weather and at least a week after bordeaux has been used in the vicinity. Use derris or quassia sprays as a last resort. *Note:* Check that the mites are still there before acting. The damage to the foliage will not disappear even when the pest is controlled.
	Symptoms:	Tiny, reddish, granular patches on stems, branches and trunk
	Cause:	Bryobia and European mite
	Solution:	Use an oil spray when trees are dormant. *See* **Red spider mite**, above.
	Symptoms:	Dimples in fruit. Do not confuse these with the depressions due to bitter pit.
	Cause:	Apple dimpling bug
	Solution:	Since the damage is only cosmetic, rely on bird and wasp predators. Spray with quassia or bug juice if you must.
	Symptoms:	Shrivelled shoots; tunnels in the fruit
	Cause:	Oriental fruit moth
	Solution:	Rely on wasp predators if possible. Cut off affected twigs. Remove and destroy affected fruit twice a week. Scrape any loose bark off the trunk and keep all rubbish away from it. From December onward keep cardboard or hessian bands around the tree and collect the sheltering insects every two days. *See* **Codling moth**, pp.88-90 for preventative techniques.

orm damage to a potato

Brown rot attacking an orange

on a peach

An apple damaged by sunburn

mato suffering from blossom end rot

Brown rot on a peach

Celery afflicted by bacteria soft rot

Damage caused by a codling moth

Post harvest fungal attack on kiwi fruit

Evidence of the apple dimpling bug

Fruit-fly sting on an orange

A nectarine suffering from shot hole

anium foliage eaten by snails

Orange tree leaves harbouring scale

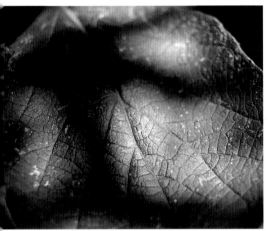

e damage on a kiwi fruit leaf

Grasshopper damage to peach foliage

f spot on fucshia leaves

Blackberry rust

A young citrus bug on an orange tree leaf

Yellowed violets suffering from overcrowding and slug an mite attack

A yellow violet leaf — indication of root rot

Leaf blister mite on a grapevine

Apple foliage attacked by leafminers

Damage caused by pear and cherry slugs

PROBLEMS		
Apples (continued)	Symptoms:	Wilted branches; die back of the tree, either sudden or gradual
	Cause:	Fruit tree weevil
	Solution:	Remove all branches that overhang the soil and grease-band the trunk and branches. The larvae pupate in the soil and the weevil climbs up into the tree to breed. Aim to break the breeding cycle.
	Symptoms:	Failure to fruit
	Cause:	Unwise pruning; a warm winter; codling moth; fluctuating water supply and poor pollination
	Solution:	Apples fruit on older spurs, and heavy pruning can lead to excessive foliage and too little blossom and fruit. There is nothing to be done about winter temperature but you can take steps against codling moth. *See* **Codling moth** pp.88-90. Good gardening techniques should take care of the last two reasons.
Apricots	Symptoms:	Failure to fruit
	Cause:	Tree may be too young; the winter may have been too warm or late frosts may have killed the blossom; silver-eyes, bowerbirds and parrots may have eaten small fruit and blossom; pruning may have been too heavy.
	Solution:	There is no need to prune apricots.
	Symptoms:	Leaves and twigs in top branches yellow and finally die
	Cause:	Verticillium fungus, 'black heart'
	Solution:	Do not grow apricots near tomatoes, capsicums or potatoes as the spores of the fungus can transfer from them to the trees. If in doubt about the ground where you wish to plant apricots, cover it with clear plastic and leave for three weeks to destroy the fungus.
	Symptoms:	Withered shoots and blossom
	Cause:	Frost damage
	Solution:	Cover the ground around the trees with a thick mulch before it heats up; keeping the soil cool will delay flowering until frosts are over. Large unpruned trees are less susceptible to frost than pruned ones.

PROBLEMS		
Apricots (continued)	Symptoms:	Fruit is covered with a brown rot and, sometimes, grey spores; flowers die, particularly if the year is a wet one
	Cause:	Brown rot
	Solution:	Spray regularly with seaweed to increase resistance to brown rot. Spray with chamomile or chives every two days or garlic once a week until all the fruit is picked. Thin fruit out so that they do not touch and remove any infected fruit immediately. Prune off all dead wood, twigs and mummified fruit when tree is dormant. Spray with bordeaux in winter. In a bad case, spray at leaf-fall and bud-swell too.
	Symptoms:	Small brown-ringed holes in leaves; fruit covered with small red blotches
	Cause:	Shot-hole
	Solution:	As for **brown rot** above
	Symptoms:	Scabby patches on fruit, which may crack
	Cause:	Apricot freckle
	Solution:	As for **brown rot** above
	Symptoms:	Grey splotches on leaves and gum oozing from trunk and branches
	Cause:	Bacterial gummosis
	Solution:	Spray with bordeaux in winter. Prune as little as possible and keep the secateurs disinfected by dipping them in vinegar before you move on to the next tree.
	Symptoms:	Branches die back
	Cause:	Dead-arm disease
	Solution:	Never prune in wet weather or with secateurs that have not been disinfected. Prune only in summer when wounds can heal quickly.
	Symptoms:	Brown patches on fruit, rotten, maggot ridden insides
	Cause:	Fruit-fly
	Solution:	*See* **Fruit-fly**, pp.87-88

PROBLEMS		
Apricots (continued)	Symptoms:	Chewed or webbed leaves, fruit tunnelled from the outside
	Cause:	Light brown apple moth
	Solution:	Remove neighbouring weeds. Encourage natural predators — birds, spiders and wasps. Spray with Dipel.
	Symptoms:	Poor fruit-set
	Cause:	Severe late frosts, waterlogging, fluctuating moisture levels, lack of bees or damage by birds; a warm winter
	Solution:	Improve gardening technique. If winters in your area are mild, choose a variety which requires fewer freeze hours.
Avocados	Symptoms:	Failure to fruit
	Cause:	Tree is too young or has been grown from seed; poor pollination; frost damage
	Solution:	Buy grafted trees. Plant two trees to help ensure pollination. Spray with seaweed to increase resistance to frost and provide protection against wind at flowering time.
	Symptoms:	Leaves yellow, tree dies back from the top
	Cause:	*Phytophthora* root rot and other root rots
	Solution:	Keep soil around trees moist but never waterlogged and the pH around 6. Add a sprinkle of lime and some hen manure once a year to keep up the phosphorus level of the soil. Do not dig around the trees. Mulch with compost, comfrey, lucerne or cow manure with a little blood and bone, or old hen manure — anything is better than nothing. Cut back dying wood to healthy tissue and use a foliar spray of green manure (*See* **Recipes for pest and disease control**, p.137.) Every two days to give the nutrients needed for survival until the root system re-establishes itself.

PROBLEMS

Avocados	Symptoms:	Wilted or deformed leaves; sooty mould
(continued)	Cause:	Aphids
	Solution:	Get rid of the weeds that host the aphids. Plant marigolds, tansy or wormwood near the tree. Grease band the trunk to prevent ants from climbing up. Wait three weeks for birds, wasps, hoverflies, lacewings and ladybirds and their larvae to deal with the pests. Blast aphids off with strong jets of water. Use a dilute clay, nettle, wormwood or seaweed spray. Resort to sprays of either garlic, onion, derris, lantana or rhubarb leaf if pests prove intractable. A baking soda and soap spray is useful in winter. *See* **Recipes for pest and disease control**, p.137. Covering the ground around the trees with reflective foil can work in bad cases.
	Symptoms:	Wilted new growth, sooty mould, red areas on fruit; a mass of small scales
	Cause:	San José scale
	Solution:	Crush the scale between your fingers and leave it on the tree to attract predators — ladybirds, lacewings, birds (especially pardalotes) and certain wasps. Use a dilute clay spray at any time. Pyrethrum, quassia and garlic sprays will kill both pest and predator so use only if you must. Use an oil spray or a washing soda spray in late winter or early spring but not if the trees are flowering or the temperature is above 24ºC; use a soapy spray in the late evening instead, drenching the leaves but not touching the flowers. Bordeaux will kill the beneficient predators; never use it in spring. If you *have* to use it, spray alternate trees, then do the rest 10 days later. Grease-band the base of the trees. Do not use orange, japonica, hawthorn or tree lucerne as windbreaks — they all harbour the scale.

PROBLEMS		
Avocados (continued)	Symptoms: Cause: Solution:	Distorted leaves and flowers; premature leaf-drop; small black droppings Thrips; some thrips are useful predators Wait for rain or hot dry weather to reduce numbers. Wasps, lacewings and ladybirds will clear the problem naturally. Try strong jets of water, preferably hot, or a soapy water spray. Use either a dilute clay, onion or derris spray as a last resort. An oil and pyrethrum spray may be used in winter if thrips have been present during the previous season. *Warning:* Do not use oil sprays and bordeaux within a week of each other.
	Symptoms: Cause: Solution:	Rotten, maggot ridden fruit Fruit-fly *See* **Fruit-fly**, pp.87-88
	Symptoms: Cause: Solution:	Dark blotches on fruit Anthracnose fungus Prune out all dead wood; spray with bordeaux.
	Symptoms: Cause: Solution:	Fruit stems rot Stem-end rot Clip the fruit from the branch, leaving a short stalk. Do not pull or twist or you may damage the joint betwen stem and fruit. Avocado picking is an art.
	Symptoms: Cause: Solution:	Yellow or red streaks on fruit, bark and leaves Sun-blotch virus Dig out infected trees and burn; there is no cure.
	Symptoms: Cause: Solution:	Blemished fruit Damage from sun, hail or by rubbing against other fruit or branches Arrange the ripening fruit to avoid rubbing; protect the trees by growing bananas, non-encroaching bamboo, trellised kiwifruit, passionfruit, or sugarcane as a screen.

PROBLEMS		
Avocados (continued)	Symptoms: Cause: Solution:	Failure to set fruit Waterlogging; too many dry spells of weather; fluctuating water levels; strong, cold winds when fruit is setting; poor pollination Check drainage; keep tree watered but not overwatered. Check your variety, some trees need another tree growing nearby to ensure pollination. Make sure there are plenty of flowers growing nearby to attract bees. Keep bees yourself. If you live in a cold area, give fortnightly sprays of seaweed to help fruit to set.
	Symptoms: Cause: Solution:	Leaves fall Possible root-rot If the tree wobbles, you have a problem. *See* **Root-rots**, pp.99-100. Young trees may need temporary shelter against the sun. Make hessian shelters or grow bananas or trellised passionfruit or kiwifruit nearby.
Bananas	Symptoms: Cause: Solution:	Failure to fruit Cool weather; bad gardening techniques Do not allow too many suckers after the initial bunch of bananas appears. Feed with compost, old hen manure and plenty of water while tree is fruiting.
	Symptoms: Cause: Solution:	Grubs in the suckers Banana weevil borer Keep base of tree free from debris and weeds.
Blueberries	Symptoms: Cause: Solution:	Split berries Overhead watering Mulch well. Do not overhead water.
	Symptoms: Cause: Solution:	Grey mould and spots on leaves and fruit Grey mould and leaf-spot Cut off and burn all infected fruit and foliage. Spray with chamomile or casuarina every few days as soon as symptoms appear. Keep bushes well mulched and spray with bordeaux when they are dormant.

PROBLEMS		
Blueberries (continued)	Symptoms:	Chewed leaves
	Cause:	Caterpillars, especially those of the light brown apple moth
	Solution:	Encourage spiders, birds and wasps — the natural predators. Dust leaves with ground rock sulphate; spray with white pepper or Dipel. *See* **Recipes for pest and disease control**, p.137. If damage is great, spray with garlic or pyrethrum.
Cherries	Symptoms:	Split fruit
	Cause:	Too much rain or watering and too much high-nitrogen fertiliser
	Solution:	Do not overhead water. Keep soil moist, never too dry or waterlogged. Mow the grass around the trees. Do not mulch them — mulching will slow down the fruiting. Cherries need very little pruning, so stay your hand. Do not give high-nitrogen fertiliser; a scatter of blood and bone or old hen manure around the tree once a year on the mown grass is all the trees need. Cherries die of too much care more readily than of neglect.
	Symptoms:	Sickly trees with signs of dieback; folded leaves
	Cause:	Fruit tree root weevil. The larvae of the weevil tunnel into the roots; the adults eat the leaves and stems, lay eggs in the leaves and fold them over.
	Solution:	Break the breeding cycle. Do not let heavily laden branches touch the soil or weeds growing around the tree. Make a fly-wire or hessian 'skirt' around the base of the tree to catch the adults as they emerge from the soil.
	Symptoms:	Holes in the trunk; sawdust indicates a continuing presence of the pest.
	Cause:	Wood-burrowing moths
	Solution:	Poke the larvae out of the holes or inject pyrethrum into the holes. Fill holes with grafting wax or putty.

PROBLEMS		
Cherries (continued)	Symptoms: Cause: Solution:	Dark, splitting wood; dead wood exuding gum Bacterial canker Prune as little as possible; canker usually starts from pruning wounds. Only prune to limit height, and in winter when tree is dormant. Spray with bordeaux just before or after pruning.
	Symptoms: Cause: Solution:	Dark, soft patches on fruit Brown rot Do not overhead water while fruit is ripening. Spray with chamomile tea every few days while the fruit is ripening. Spray with bordeaux in winter.
	Symptoms: Cause: Solution:	Skeletonised leaves and possible defoliation Pear and cherry slug Vigorous trees can tolerate some damage, so encourage bird and wasp predators and otherwise ignore the pest and do not worry. Dust leaves with dry wood ash or flour browned in the oven to suffocate the pests. Use derris or pyrethrum spray or Dipel, but only use if pests are visible before fruit ripens. Do not grow hawthorn nearby.
Boysenberries		*See* Raspberries
Chestnuts		*See* Walnuts
Citrus trees	Symptoms: Cause: Solution:	Failure to fruit Too young; frost at flowering time; poor pollination; fluctuating water supply; unwise feeding Protect trees against frost if necessary; encourage bees to ensure pollination; keep up a steady water supply. The trees probably have been fed with too much nitrogen and too little phosphorus. Dress the ground around the trees with rock-phosphate while you amend your feeding programme. Use a good mulch containing blood and bone, some old hen manure or well-made compost.

PROBLEMS

Citrus trees (continued)	Symptoms:	Thick rind on the fruit
	Cause:	Thick rind is common in young trees and will lessen as the trees age; if old trees have thick-skinned fruit, they are getting too much nitrogen.
	Solution:	Add some ground rock phosphate to the soil around the trees as a temporary measure while you mend the feeding programme to good-quality mulch containing some blood and bone or old hen manure. Over-ripe Valencias have a thick rind and so do some grapefruit growing in cold areas.
	Symptoms:	Brown centres to the fruit
	Cause:	Boron deficiency, possibly precipitated by very dry or very wet weather
	Solution:	Correct your feeding regime and use liquid fertiliser as a foliar spray in the interim. *See* **Recipes for pest and disease control**, p.137.
	Symptoms:	Small puncture hole in fruit, which has a rotten, maggot ridden centre
	Cause:	Fruit-fly
	Solution:	*See* **Fruit-fly**, pp.87-88.
	Symptoms: Cause: Solution:	Small insects on new shoots Aphids Grow wormwood, tansy, marigolds or lavender nearby as a deterrent. Spray with Vegemite dissolved in water to attract natural predators. Put down reflective foil on the soil around the plants. Wait three weeks for natural predators to build up before spraying with either dilute clay, nettle, wormwood or seaweed. As a last resort use a derris, rhubarb leaf or garlic spray. In cold weather use a baking soda spray.
	Symptoms:	Clusters of small brown spots on leaves, worse after autumn rain
	Cause:	Brown or septoria rot
	Solution:	Use seaweed spray or a plant tonic every three weeks as a preventative. *See* **Recipes for pest and disease control**, p.137. Use chamomile spray after rain and bordeaux spray in autumn.

PROBLEMS		
Citrus trees (continued)	Symptoms: Cause: Solution:	Sunken brown or black spots on fruit Black spot *See* **Brown or septoria rot**, p.65
	Symptoms: Cause: Solution:	Shoots and even branches wilt; tree becomes sickly Bugs, stink or horned Clear away weeds around the tree; clear away old pots, wood heaps, broken-down fences near the tree — they can all harbour the bugs. Put down reflective foil between the trees to deter the adult bugs. Encourage wasps, lady-birds, parasitic fungi and lacewing and hoverfly larvae, all of which feed on the bugs. Pick off and kill bugs by hand. **Wear gloves and keep your face away.** The bugs jet out a stinging, acrid fluid when disturbed. Jet the bugs off the tree with water directed all over the tree but especially under the leaves. Shake the trees and stamp on the fallen bugs. Put cardboard shelters or pieces of hose around affected trees and check every day to see if bugs are sheltering there. As a last resort, use garlic, wormwood, pyrethrum or rhubarb leaf spray on the leaves the bug will eat, not the bugs themselves. The effect will last only for a few days so you will have to keep it up.
	Symptoms: Cause: Solution:	Small red scabs on fruit Red scale Do not use sprays which might kill the natural predators. Use an oil spray when temperature is under 24°C. Try dilute clay, onion or pyrethrum spray.
	Symptoms: Solution:	Tree dies back; bark is lifted at the base of the tree; foliage yellows Cut out all dead wood and bark. Paint wounds with bordeaux paste. Keep grass and mulch at least 10 cm away from the trunk to avoid mowing injury or water puddling around it.
	Symptoms: Cause: Solution:	Misshapen or 'horned' fruit with scabby top Lemon scab, a fungus which attacks the fruit soon after it has set. Spray at petal-fall with either a one in 10 diluted urine mixture or bordeaux.

PROBLEMS		
Citrus trees (continued)	Symptoms:	Trees dies back; foliage yellows, dulls and starts to die, often on one side of the tree only
	Cause:	Root-rots (*phytophthora, citriodora* and others)
	Solution:	Since the trouble is worse in wet weather, it may improve as the soil dries out. Channel all water away from the trees and improve the general drainage in the area. Add thick mulch to keep up the humus level of the soil and use compost, which can inhibit root-rots. In bad cases, cut the tree back to healthy wood and use a foliar spray as a food till the tree begins to regain health. Be warned — you may think you have controlled the rot with compost but, if the weather is wet and the compost supply is not continued you will be in trouble again.
	Symptoms:	Round galls on the branches
	Cause:	The tunnelling of gall-wasp larvae
	Solution:	Cut out the galls and burn them. Encourage bird, ant and spider predators.
Currants	Symptoms:	Pale leaves
	Cause:	Shortage of potash
	Solution:	Sprinkle wood ash around the bushes every year. Mulch with compost or lucerne, or add well-rotted hen manure or some blood and bone to the soil. Black currants need more nitrogen than red or white ones.
	Symptoms:	Failure to set fruit
	Cause:	Winter was too warm.
	Symptoms:	Stems die
	Cause:	Currant borer
	Solution:	Pick off infected stems and burn them to stop the depredation spreading. Control is difficult as the caterpillars burrow into the stems where they cannot be reached by sprays.

PROBLEMS		
Currants (continued)	Symptoms:	Enlarged and distorted buds which fail to develop
	Cause:	Bud or gall mites
	Solution:	Cut off buds and burn them. Spray the bush with elder or double strength garlic at once and with bordeaux in winter.
	Symptoms:	Dark, shrivelled buds
	Cause:	Eelworm
	Solution:	Remove and burn buds. Mulch bushes well, preferably with compost.
	Symptoms:	Rotting leaves
	Cause:	Septoria leaf-rot and other fungal diseases
	Solution:	Pick off and burn leaves at first sign of trouble. Spray with milk, chamomile, casuarina or elder when the bush is in leaf and with bordeaux when it is dormant.
Custard apples	Symptoms:	Water-soaked blotching on fruit
	Cause:	Bugs
	Solution:	Control weeds. Prune off low-hanging branches, place traps made from folded hessian at the base of the trees and empty every day.
Feijoa	Symptoms:	Hole in side of fruit, rotting, maggot ridden centres
	Cause:	Fruit-fly
	Solution:	*See* **Fruit-fly**, pp.87-88
Figs	Symptoms:	Holes in trunk or branches with sawdust visible
	Cause:	Borers
	Solution:	Using a piece of wire, poke the borer out of the hole or inject pyrethrum to kill it, then fill the hole with bordeaux paste or putty. Do all the holes. Spray with bordeaux to prevent the moth from laying her eggs in the tree. *Late fruit:* If you get a late second crop of fruit, cover them in sacking as protection against frost. If it is clear that they will not ripen, remove them or they will inhibit the next crop.

PROBLEMS		
Gooseberries	Symptoms:	Leaves become yellow, webbed or dried out
	Cause:	Mites
	Solution:	Do not allow weeds near the bushes, particularly capeweed and clover. Burn all affected leaves. Encourage lacewings, ladybirds and birds. Use a milk or oil spray in early summer, a soapy water spray when it is cooler or in the evening. A dilute clay spray may help.
	Symptoms:	Grey film on foliage
	Cause:	Powdery mildew
	Solution:	Open top of bushes by careful pruning to let in air and light. Spray leaves with chamomile, casuarina or elder. Spray with bordeaux when bush is dormant.
	Symptoms:	Chewed leaves
	Cause:	Caterpillars
	Solution:	Dust leaves with ground rock phosphate; spray with dilute clay or white pepper. As a last resort use a garlic, derris, pyrethrum or Dipel spray. *See* **Recipes for pest and disease control**, p.137.
Grapefruit	Symptoms:	Premature fruit-drop
	Solution:	Keep up the water and mulch supply. Do not worry; the tree may be setting more fruit than it can sustain. For other problems, *see* **Citrus trees**
Grapes	Symptoms:	Failure to fruit
	Cause:	Powdery mildew may have affected the flowers; pruning may have been too heavy — remember that grapes grow on last year's wood.
	Solution:	Spray with bordeaux in winter.
	Symptoms:	Downy white infestation on leaves
	Cause:	Mealy bugs and Rutherglen bugs
	Solution:	Encourage birds. Remove all weeds around the vine. Mulch soil well. Spray leaves, not bugs, with pyrethrum or rhubarb leaf spray. The poison has to be eaten. Make traps of rolled-up cardboard or hessian, place under vines and check for pests every day.

PROBLEMS		
Grapes (continued)	Symptoms:	Webbed, yellowed or dried-out leaves
	Cause:	Mites
	Solution:	Check that the mites are still there before acting — the damage to the foliage does not disappear even when the pest is controlled. Remove weeds — mulch over them or slash them. Use overhead watering in hot dry weather to discourage red spider mites. Large orchards sometimes purchase predator mites, *Typhlodromus occidentalis*. They are only useful for large areas as they need a large supply of mites to survive. Try milk, coriander or anise spray. Oil sprays are effective but should not be used in hot weather or within a week of using bordeaux. Onion and garlic sprays are effective but will kill predators too. Use derris or quassia spray as a last resort.
	Symptoms:	Tunnels burrowed into the canes
	Cause:	Vine and elephant weevil
	Solution:	Cut out affected canes and burn them.
	Symptoms:	Galls on the roots
	Cause:	Phylloxera
	Solution:	Control aphids. Grow vines only from resistant stock. Contact the Department of Agriculture for information about the areas where phylloxera is prevalent.
	Symptoms:	Rotting or withered fruit; flowers that fail to fruit; powdery deposits on vines
	Cause:	Fungal mould and mildew disease of fruit and foliage
	Solution:	Do not overhead water; mulch well. Space out laterals and make certain plenty of air is circulating around the vines. Dust leaves lightly with powdered sulphur as soon as conditions appear. Spray with chamomile, casuarina, elder or double strength garlic. Spray with bordeaux in autumn and at bud-burst.
	Symptoms:	Reddish purple mottling, yellow blotches affect the leaves; canes are deformed
	Cause:	Viral disease
	Solution:	Dig out canes at once and burn them. There is no cure.

PROBLEMS		
Hazelnuts	Symptoms:	Small insects clustered on new shoots
	Cause:	Aphids
	Solution:	Grow wormwood, tansy or nasturtium under the trees. Place reflective foil on the ground between the trees. Try a wormwood, garlic or rhubarb leaf spray.
	Symptoms:	Grey film on leaves
	Cause:	Mildew and hazelnut blight
	Solution:	Use a bordeaux spray in winter. Mulch well and do not grow anything between the bushes.
Kiwifruit	Symptoms:	Chewed leaves and fruit
	Cause:	Light brown apple moth and other moths
	Solution:	Dust leaves with white pepper. Spray with garlic or Dipel. Encourage birds and wasps. *See* **Apples.**
Lemons		*See* Citrus trees
Limes	Symptoms:	Fruit is scabby and leaves develop yellow patches with brown blotches
	Cause:	Melanose. Limes are more subject to melanose than other citrus.
	Solution:	Spray with bordeaux at petal-fall. Cut out all dead wood and remove every weed near the tree. Mulch heavily. Renew the mulch every six months.
Loganberries		*See* Raspberries
Loquats	Symptoms:	Brown patches on fruit, centres maggot ridden
	Cause:	Fruit-fly
	Solution:	*See* **Fruit-fly**, pp.87-88
	Symptoms:	Failure to fruit
	Cause:	Loquats grown from seedlings can take 15 years to bear fruit. Loquats crop well only every second year.
	Solution:	Be patient, or grow only from grafted trees. Thin out fruit each fruiting year to try and even the production of fruit.

PROBLEMS		
Loquats (continued)	Symptoms:	Raised scabby spots on fruit
	Cause:	Scab
	Solution:	Spray with a solution of one to 10 urine and water. Spray with half strength bordeaux in autumn.
Lychee	Symptoms:	Cracked fruit
	Cause:	Dry air
	Solution:	Use microjets or sprinklers to keep up the humidity around the fruit. Keep the area crowded with foliage.
	Symptoms:	Fruit disappears
	Cause:	Fruit bats
	Solution:	Use tape-recorded loud noises as a deterrent. Net the fruit with a special fruit bat netting.
	Symptoms:	Hole in fruit with rotted, maggot ridden centres
	Cause:	Fruit-fly
	Solution:	*See* **Fruit-fly**, pp.87-88
	Symptoms:	Flowers fall; small red felt-like patches under leaves
	Cause:	Mites
	Solution:	*See* **Gooseberries.**
Macadamia nuts	Symptoms:	Dead or rotting wood at base of the tree
	Cause:	Root-rot; *Phytophthora cinnamoni* wood rot
	Solution:	Cut out infected areas and paint cuts with bordeaux paste. Make sure the soil is well drained and rich in organic matter. Keep up the mulch.
	Symptoms:	New shoots die; sawdust deposits on branches or around the tree
	Cause:	Borers
	Solution:	Cut off affected shoots and burn. Spray tree with pyrethrum and soapy water.

PROBLEMS			
Mandarins	Symptoms:		Dry and tasteless fruit
	Cause:		Fruit left on tree too long; most mandarins are over-ripe when they become bright orange.
	Symptoms:		Poor fruit yield
	Cause:		Mandarins crop well only every second year.
	Solution:		Thin very heavy crops. In years when fruit is scarce, leave some on the tree to inhibit excessive fruit formation the following year.
Mango	Symptoms:		Failure to fruit
	Cause:		Rain at flowering time
	Solution:		Spray with chamomile, casuarina or chives once every two days after rain.
	Symptoms:		Small hole in fruit, rotten, maggot ridden centres
	Cause:		Fruit-fly
	Solution:		*See* **Fruit-fly**, pp.87-88
	Symptoms:		Powdery deposits on leaves
	Cause:		Powdery mildew
	Solution:		Spray with elder, chamomile, horseradish or garlic at any time. Spray with bordeaux at petal-fall.
	Symptoms:		Sooty mould on leaves
	Cause:		Aphids; the mould is on their sugary secretions
	Solution:		Spray with white oil if the temperature is under 24ºC, or with soapy water in the cool of the evening. The mould should peel off by itself or you can wipe it off. *See* 'Aphids' under **Avocados**.
	Symptoms:		Fruit rotted at stalk-end
	Cause:		Anthracnose stem-rot
	Solution:		Pick fruit with stem on. Do not twist the stem or you may damage the junction with the branch.

PROBLEMS		
Medlar	Symptoms:	Cracked fruit
	Cause:	Poor drainage around tree; watered too often
	Solution:	Improve drainage
Mulberries	Symptoms:	Dead bark and wood at ground level
	Cause:	Collar-rot
	Solution:	Keep mulch away from the trunk. An occasional scattering of blood and bone and keeping the grass around the tree mown is all the attention a mulberry needs.
	Symptoms:	Dark, splitting bark; dead wood
	Cause:	Canker
	Solution:	Since canker enters through a wound, keep pruning to a minimum. Do it when the tree is dormant and spray with bordeaux just before or afterwards.
	Symptoms:	Young shoots die back; leaves develop brown spots with a spreading yellow halo
	Cause:	Bacterial blight
	Solution:	Remove and burn all dead wood and 'mummies'. Improve the drainage around the tree. In mild conditions spray with bordeaux when trees are dormant; in more severe cases spray at leaf-fall and bud-swell too.
Nectarines		*See* Peaches
Olives	Symptoms:	Failure to fruit
	Cause:	Have you chosen the wrong type? The African olive — the hedging one with glossy foliage — never bears fruit larger than a small pea. Olives like cold winters and hot dry summers, but not humidity. An old tree needs heavy pruning.
	Solution:	Make certain to plant the European olive, recognisable by new growth of bluish grey. Give old trees a very hard cutting back.

PROBLEMS		
Olives (continued)	Symptoms: Cause: Solution:	Brownish scaly patches on leaves Brown olive scale Jet scales off with water if they are damaging the tree, otherwise leave them to their natural predators — olives are tough trees. Use a light oil spray if temperature is under 24°C, or soapy water in the cool of the evening. Do not encourage soft sappy growth by using high-nitrogen fertiliser.
	Symptoms: Cause: Solution:	Suckers Too much nitrogen in the soil; heavy pruning; the variety may be prone to suckering. Cut down on pruning and high-nitrogen food.
Oranges	Symptoms: Solution:	Green-coloured Valencias Do not worry. The bright orange ones for sale have been treated. If home grown Valencias are bright orange they are over-ripe. *See* Citrus trees.
Passionfruit	Symptoms: Cause: Solution:	Failure to set fruit Pollen has dried out in the heat; blossoms have rotted in the humidity Keep up the balance of phosphorus. Sprinkle soil around the vine with ground rock phosphate. Prune back new growth. Do not overfeed with nitrogen.
	Symptoms: Cause: Solution:	Vine wilts; stem rots at ground level Fusarium wilt Paint the base of the stem with bordeaux paste. Spray soil around the plant with double strength garlic. Before planting a passionfruit vine, keep the planting area covered with clear plastic for three weeks to ensure pathogens in the soil are killed. Only buy passionfruit vines which have been grafted on to wilt-resistant stock. Add wood ash or compost to the soil to provide potash which will give greater resistance to wilt.
	Symptoms: Cause:	Scabby patch on skin Fruit-fly; the larvae find the skin too difficult to penetrate

PROBLEMS

Passionfruit (continued)	Symptoms: Cause: Solution:	Raised scabby or thin, shell-like patch on the fruit Green shield bugs Pick off bugs and squash them. In bad cases spray pyrethrum, derris or bug juice. *See* **Recipes for pest and disease control**, p.137 and 'Bugs' under **Citrus trees**.
	Symptoms: Cause: Solution:	Leaves wilt; fruit shrivels; sooty mould Passionvine hopper, a small brown moth with transparent wings which lays its eggs in the vine shoots Cut off affected shoots; spray with pyrethrum, derris or garlic.
	Symptoms: Cause: Solution:	Thickened rind, dry fruit, mottled leaves Virus Dig out and burn infected vines. Do not replant a vine in the same spot and sterilise any implements used.
Pawpaws	Symptoms: Cause: Solution:	Trees die back from the top Unknown Cut the tree back to healthy tissue and hope for the best.
	Symptoms: Cause: Solution:	Powdery film on leaves Mildew Spray with wettable sulphur, elder, casuarina or lilac. Cut off all infected leaves.
Peaches	Symptoms: Cause: Solution:	Pink or green blisters on leaves Curly leaf fungus The condition can be prevented but not cured. The blisters are ugly but not harmful. Unfortunately, the fungus which causes the trouble also causes premature fruit-drop. Pick off all affected leaves. Spray with chamomile, casuarina or horsetail tea once a week for three weeks. Spray with bordeaux in winter as a preventative. Be particularly vigilant in wet weather. Planting garlic under the tree may inhibit the growth of the fungus if the tops are picked often.

PROBLEMS		
Peaches (continued)	Symptoms:	Brown spots on leaves
	Cause:	Peach rust
	Solution:	Spray with bordeaux when trees are dormant.
	Symptoms:	Brown or powdery rotted fruit
	Cause:	Brown rot
	Solution:	Use seaweed spray throughout the year or bordeaux in winter to help prevent rot. In wet years, or if there is any sign of rot, spray with casuarina, horsetail or chamomile tea every few days until all the fruit is picked. Do not allow fruit to be too crowded on the branches — thin out. Pick off all dead twigs and fruit 'mummies' in winter.
	Symptoms:	Gum exudes from trunk or branches
	Cause:	Bacterial gummosis
	Solution:	Spray with bordeaux in winter, particularly before or after pruning. Sterilise secateurs after pruning each tree and before moving on to the next.
	Symptoms:	Dark, cracked bark; dead wood
	Cause:	Canker
	Solution:	Spray with bordeaux in winter, just before or after pruning. Keep wounds as small as possible and do not allow one branch to rub against another. After pruning one tree, sterilise the secateurs before moving on to the next.
	Symptoms:	Unusual leaf or growth patterns
	Cause:	Virus
	Solution:	Regular use of seaweed spray is said to make peaches more resistant to viruses, but, unfortunately, there is no cure.
	Symptoms:	Broken branches
	Cause:	Vase-shaped pruning; letting heavily laden branches take the full weight of the fruit.
	Solution:	Prune carefully. Prop up heavily laden branches with wooden stakes or loop rope around them and secure it to the main trunk.

PROBLEMS		
Pears	Symptoms:	Fruit drops
	Cause:	Poor pollination; soil too dry
	Solution:	Make sure the varieties you are growing pollinate each other. Keep soil moist and water regularly, Grow flowers to attract bees. Take up bee-keeping; convince your neighbours not to use pesticides.
	Symptoms:	Rotting fruit
	Cause:	Bruising due to clumsy handling during picking
	Solution:	Always handle pears carefully.
	Symptoms:	Small scales on stems and leaves
	Cause:	Scale
	Solution:	Grease-band the trees to deter ants. Use a dilute clay spray. If that fails use pyrethrum or garlic.
	Symptoms:	Leaves become yellowed, webbed or dried-out
	Cause:	Mites
	Solution:	Check that the mites are still there before acting. The damage they do to the foliage does not disappear even when the pest is controlled. Control weeds — mulch over or slash them. Use overhead watering in hot dry weather to discourage red spider mites. Large orchards sometimes purchase predator mites *Typhlodromus occidentalis*. They are useful only for large areas as they need a large supply of mites to survive. Try milk, coriander or anise spray. Oil sprays are effective but should not be used in hot weather or within a week of using bordeaux. Onion and garlic sprays are effective but will kill predators too. Use derris or quassia sprays as a last resort.
	Symptoms:	Web-like patterns on leaves; defoliation
	Cause:	Pear and cherry slug
	Solution:	Dust leaves with dry wood ash or flour browned in the oven. Spray with derris or pyrethrum. Encourage birds and wasps which are natural predators. Do not grow near a hawthorn hedge.

PROBLEMS		
Pecan	Symptoms:	Premature fruit-fall
	Solution:	Keep moisture level of the soil even — no drying out and compensating flooding. Feed the tree adequately.
	Symptoms:	Holes in the nuts
	Cause:	Wood borers and peach-moth borers
	Solution:	*See* **Codling moth** pp.88-90
Persimmons	Symptoms:	Failure to set fruit
	Cause:	A dry spring or too much nitrogen in the food. The tree may be an old variety which requires a male tree for fertilisation
	Solution:	Plant only modern varieties which are self-pollinating. Adjust feeding. Check to make sure certain birds are not taking the fruit as soon as it has set.
	Symptoms:	Sharp-tasting fruit
	Cause:	Tree is an old variety. New varieties are less tart
	Symptoms:	Fruit falls prematurely
	Cause:	Fluctuating moisture levels of the soil; pruning
	Solution:	Keep the tree well watered. Never prune it — all you will do is to ruin its beautiful shape.
	Symptoms:	Tree sickens
	Cause:	Root-rot
	Solution:	Keep soil well drained. Use compost liberally as a mulch. Do not use high-nitrogen fertiliser. Feed with compost and a sprinkle of dolomite each year.
	Symptoms:	Hole in side of fruit; rotten, maggot ridden centres
	Cause:	Fruit-fly
	Solution:	Persimmons are subject to fruit-fly only in warm areas where the pests survive the winters. *See* **Fruit-fly**, pp.87-88

PROBLEMS		
Pineapple	Symptoms: Solution:	Root-rot Ensure good drainage around the plants. Mulch. Keep plants growing strongly. *See* **Root-rots**, pp.99-100
	Symptoms: Cause: Solution:	Tiny, waxy ovals on wilting leaves and shoots Mealy bugs Their protective coating means that pesticides are not much use against mealy bugs. Try oil spray if the temperature is under 24°C, or soapy water in the cool of the evening. Encourage the natural predators — ladybirds, lacewing larvae and chalcid parasitic wasps. Grease-band the base of the trees to discourage ants which bring the pests.
	Cause: Solution:	Eelworm (nematodes) Mulch soil and keep up levels of organic matter in it, especially if soil is sandy. Compost inhibits nematodes. Grow a companion crop of marigolds.
Plums	Symptoms: Cause: Solution:	Hole in side of fruit, rotten, maggot ridden centres Fruit-fly *See* **Fruit-fly**, pp.87-88
	Symptoms: Cause: Solution:	Skeletonised leaves Pear and cherry slug Encourage the natural predators — birds and wasps. Dust leaves with dry wood ash or flour browned in the oven to suffocate the pests. Spray with derris, pyrethrum or Dipel.
	Symptoms: Cause: Solution:	Chewed leaves; fruit tunnelled from the outside Light brown apple moth Encourage the natural predators — birds, spiders and wasps. Do not use pesticides.

PROBLEMS

Plums (continued)		
	Symptoms:	Distorted leaves and flowers; small black droppings
	Cause:	Mites
	Solution:	Control weeds. Use milk, coriander, anise or garlic spray at any time; use an oil spray in cool weather and derris as a last resort. Remember that the damage remains even when pest is controlled.
	Symptoms:	Scale-like encrustations on leaves
	Cause:	San José scale
	Solution:	Spray with white oil if temperature is under 24°C. If you must use bordeaux — which kills natural predators — spray alternate trees and do the rest a week later. Do not plant plums near tree lucerne or hawthorn hedges.
	Symptoms:	Powdery spots under leaves
	Cause:	Prune rust
	Solution:	Spray with bordeaux at bud-swell.
	Symptoms:	Light green spots on leaves and small, scabby, cracked spots on fruit
	Cause:	Bacterial spot
	Solution:	Spray with bordeaux at bud-swell. Spray leaves with elder, lilac, chamomile or casuarina to stop infection spreading.
	Symptoms:	Small holes in the leaves
	Cause:	Shot-hole
	Solution:	Spray with bordeaux at bud-swell.
	Symptoms:	Gum exudes from trunk or branches
	Cause:	Gummosis
	Solution:	Spray with bordeaux when trees are dormant.

PROBLEMS		
Plums (continued)	Symptoms:	Leaves turn silvery and branches rot
	Cause:	Silver leaf fungus
	Solution:	There is no cure. Prevent by not pruning in wet weather. Cover all cuts with bordeaux paste and spray with bordeaux either just before, or just after, pruning. An old remedy was to cut the bark of the tree down to the cambium layer and into the wood every year for four years, but I do not know how effective this is.
	Symptoms:	Brown rotten patches on the fruit
	Cause:	Brown rot
	Solution:	Cut off all dead twigs and 'mummies', then spray with bordeaux in winter. Thin out fruit to improve air and light penetration. Pick off all rotting fruit and spray with chamomile every two days.

Plumcot This cross between a plum and an apricot shares the problems of both trees.

Pomegranate	Symptoms:	Splitting fruit
	Cause:	Wet weather
	Solution:	Pick them when the weather is dry and they are still yellow. Let them ripen indoors. Do not over water.
Quince	Symptoms:	Black spots on leaves; cracked fruit
	Cause:	Quince fleck
	Solution:	Train trees to a single open-branched stem to make sure of adequate light penetration. Do not plant quinces in a humid, sheltered spot, such as near a fishpond or vegetable garden that is watered frequently. Burn all infected leaves. Spray with bordeaux at bud-burst and with either elder, garlic, chamomile or lilac when symptoms appear.
	Symptoms:	Hole in side of fruit; rotten, maggot ridden centre
	Cause:	Fruit-fly
	Solution:	*See* **Fruit-fly**, pp.87-88

PROBLEMS		
Quince (continued)	Symptoms: Cause: Solution:	Rotting fruit Codling moth *See* **Codling moth**, pp.88-90
Raspberries, Loganberries, Youngberries and Boysenberries	Symptoms: Cause: Solution:	Clusters of small insects on new shoots Aphids Use an oil spray in cool weather, and a wormwood spray at any time. Interplant bushes with tansy, wormwood or lavender.
	Symptoms: Cause: Solution:	Distorted leaves and flowers Thrips Spray with either dilute clay, onion, derris or soapy water.
	Symptoms: Cause: Solution:	Yellowed, mottled, dried-up leaves Mites Remove all neighbouring weeds. Spray with either anise, coriander, derris or quassia. Use an oil spray in cool weather.
	Symptoms: Cause: Solution:	Purple spots on canes Cane spot Spray with bordeaux in mid winter or half strength bordeaux at bud-swell.
	Symptoms: Cause: Solution:	Silvery-brown fungus on canes Spur blight *See* **Cane spot** above.
	Symptoms: Cause: Solution:	Rusty patches on canes Raspberry leaf rust *See* **Cane spot** above

PROBLEMS		
Raspberries, Loganberries, Youngberries, and Boysenberries (continued)	Symptoms:	Powdery deposits on leaves
	Cause:	Downy mildew
	Solution:	*See* **Cane spot**. Spray with chamomile, elder or garlic when canes are in leaf. Cut out affected leaves and burn. Always grow raspberries in thick mulch and do not give them too much nitrogen.
	Symptoms:	Hard fruit
	Cause:	Harlequin beetles which suck the fruit
	Solution:	Thin out vines and clear away debris which might harbour the beetles. Plant turnips nearby as a decoy crop. *See* 'Bugs' under **Citrus trees**.
	Symptoms:	Mouldy fruit
	Cause:	Rain
	Solution:	Pick raspberries immediately after rain; remove any mouldy ones to prevent infection and spray the rest with chamomile.
Strawberries	Symptoms:	Brown spots on leaves
	Cause:	Leaf spot fungus
	Solution:	Do not overhead water. Mulch thickly and use a hose or dripper under the mulch. Thin out to allow light and air penetration. Spray with elder, lilac, chamomile or double strength garlic. When cropping is over, spray with half strength bordeaux.
	Symptoms:	Pale, soft watery berries
	Cause:	*Botrytis* fungus
	Solution:	Prune away overlush foliage. The fungus is worst in moist, sheltered areas. Spray with lilac or chamomile, or with half strength bordeaux late at night when it is cool.
	Symptoms:	Clusters of insects on new shoots
	Cause:	Aphids
	Solution:	Spray with wormwood, derris or rhubarb leaf. Interplant with tansy, wormwood or lavender. Put down reflective foil between the plants.

PROBLEMS		
Strawberries (continued)	Symptoms: Cause: Solution:	Dull, pitted leaves Red spider mite Cover leaves with milk, anise or coriander spray. Remove all nearby weeds.
	Symptoms: Cause: Solution:	Rusty brown leaves with a fine, lacy webbing on the underside Two-spotted mite Slash weeds around affected tree or mulch over them. Overhead water when weather is hot and dry. Spray with milk, coriander or anise. Onion and garlic sprays are effective but will kill beneficial predators. Try an oil spray, in cool weather at least a week after using bordeaux.
	Symptoms: Cause: Solution:	Plants die suddenly Nematodes Use plenty of mulch, particularly if the soil is sandy. Interplant strawberries with marigolds.
	Symptoms: Cause: Solution:	Hollowed out fruit Eelworm nematodes Pick every day — eelworm like ripe strawberries. Mulch well.
Tamarillos	Symptoms: Cause: Solution:	Hole in side of fruit; rotten, maggot ridden centre Fruit-fly *See* **Fruit-fly**, pp.87-88
	Symptoms: Cause: Solution:	Plant wilts and dies — gradually or suddenly Root-rot Improve drainage around plant. Dig out plant and leave the soil open to the weather for a few months. *See* **Root-rots**, pp.99-100. Tamarillos are short-lived and easily grown from cuttings. You can bend a branch over to the soil and cover it with mulch until it develops a new root system. Make certain soil is well drained.

PROBLEMS		
Tangelos are a cross between a mandarin and a grapefruit and share their problems.		
Walnuts	Symptoms:	Black spots on leaves; black, withered nuts
	Cause:	Bacterial blight
	Solution:	Spray with bordeaux at leaf-fall and bud-swell in bad cases, otherwise just in winter.
	Symptoms:	Leaves and branches die from the tips downwards
	Cause:	Root-rot
	Solution:	Make sure drainage is good, pH of the soil is around 6, and no native trees are growing nearby. Add a sprinkle of lime and hen manure once a year to keep up the phosphorus level of the soil. Mulch with compost, comfrey, lucerne or cow manure with a little blood and bone. Do not dig around the trees.
	Symptoms:	Thin, frilly fungi on trunk and branches; dark, dead wood
	Cause:	Wood-rotting fungus
	Solution:	The fungi usually attack only dead or injured wood and waterlogged or starved trees. Take care pruning, make sure drainage is good and keep trees growing strongly. Cut out all affected wood down to healthy tissue and watch to see that healthy wood closes over the wound.

Fruit-Fly

It is possible to control fruit-fly organically. It is also a lot of work, but so is any other form of control. Two sorts of fruit-fly are common in Australia — the Queensland and the Mediterranean. Both have similar life cycles and we are required by law to keep them under control.

Prevention

In cold areas where the fruit-fly die off in winter, a total clean-up of fallen fruit could be enough to prevent the fly from building up into problem proportions for the following year. Fruit-fly mature in fallen and ripe fruit so the less of it left about the better.

In any area, fallen fruit should be picked up every day or, better still, eaten by chickens or animals browsing under the trees. Fruit-fly infected fruit falls before it is ripe and having it pass through an animal's gullet is a simple way of interrupting the breeding cycle.

Never bury infected fruit or put it into a compost heap. You can stew it and feed it to the chooks. You can put it in a bucket, cover it with water, seal the bucket and leave it for three weeks. By then it should be safe to add to the compost. You can put it in a plastic garbage bag, seal the bag and leave it in the sun for three weeks to turn it into anaerobic compost.

In bad fruit-fly areas, do not grow loquats or other fruit which ripen early. They will attract the fly to your garden so that it is already there when your main crop ripens. Late-ripening fruits such as quinces, figs and medlars can host fruit-fly and act as a breeding ground so that the pests are all ready for the winter citrus. It is a good idea to have a gap of about two months in summer between any crops the fruit-flies fancy. It will take more than that to get rid of them, but at least you will not be encouraging them. Use any time you have to clean up the orchard or garden.

Repellent

Mix together a litre of kerosene, a litre of creosote and a packet of mothballs. The mixture will stink. Pour it into a number of small tin cans and hang them, about 10 metres apart, in the fruit trees and around the garden. Hopefully, the flies won't like the smell either.

The next method of attack is the lure. Fruit-fly fly for about a week before they mate and the eggs are laid. If you can kill them during this week the breeding cycle will be broken, so this is the time to use baits and traps. You can buy Dak pots to hang around the garden but they are only effective against the male Queensland fruit-fly and it is the females which do the damage.

Splash-on bait

Mix 50 grams sugar and 7 ml concentrated pyrethrum or nicotine in one litre of water. From two weeks before to one week after the known fruit-fly dates in your district, every week, splash the mixture over the trees you wish to protect. Don't spray it on — a spray is not effective enough. Be sure to splash it over the trees every week, for pyrethrum breaks down on contact with light and nicotine remains effective only for a few days.

Traps

You can use open or closed traps. Open traps are just small containers without a lid. To make a closed trap, cut an empty plastic soft drink container in two at shoulder level. Turn the top piece upside down and insert it into the bottom part of the container so that the pouring lip is inside and tape the join securely. You then fill the bottle to about a third with one of the baits listed below and cover the hole with mosquito netting. A simpler bait is made by filling a plastic bottle half full with bait, screwing on the top, turning the bottle upside down and punching a series of holes in it. When the bottle is hung upside down, the flies get into the bottle in search of the bait but cannot get out again.

Baits

Bran, sugar and hot water

Banana peel in water

Orange peel, human urine and water

Vegemite and water

Molasses, flour and water

Vegemite, banana peel, urine and water

Fruit-fly love the sweet yeastiness of these mixtures and drown in them. Two poisonous baits, which are better used in the closed traps so that bees and wasps are not caught inadvertently, are:
one teaspoon of molasses and a pinch of pyrethrum powder in 125 ml water or 10 grams yeast with a pinch of pyrethrum powder in 125 ml water

A few drops of citronella could make the bait even more attractive. Be certain to use molasses, not honey or sugar. It is less attractive to bees.

Codling Moth

Codling moths were introduced to Australia by the settlers who brought in fruit trees from Europe. They have never found a source of food in native plants and still rely on apples and, to a lesser extent, pears, walnuts, quinces, peaches, nectarines, plums, hawthorn hips and, occasionally, eggplant for their food. Their name comes from the wild codling tree from which the modern varieties of apple are derived.

The insects lay their eggs, which look like tiny, flat, circular scales, on or near the fruit, when the temperature is around 15°C. The eggs hatch in one to two weeks, depending on temperature, and the young caterpillars enter the fruit, usually from the top or bottom, and chew their way into it. Once the caterpillar is inside the fruit eradication of the pest is difficult.

After three to five weeks the caterpillars leave the fruit and search for the butt of a tree, a dark corner of a wooden shed, old wooden fruit boxes, ladders, or any wooden object on which to spin their cocoons. The peak time for hatching is from October to December, with a following hatching in December to January. There can be even more hatchings a year and the cocoons can remain dormant for up to two years. Control of codling moth in apples like Granny Smith which take time to mature is therefore difficult.

In 1975 the CSIRO conducted an experiment in Victoria. Scientists contained 36 apple trees in wire cages from which codling moths could neither escape nor enter, conducted extensive searches and sprayed twice with ryania. It took two years to wipe out the pests. Difficult and tedious though gaining control may be, once it is

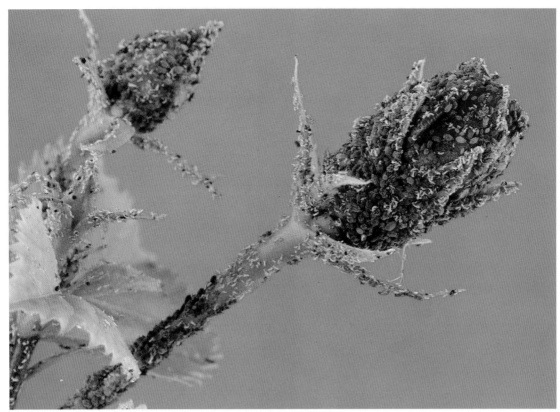

Aphid infestation being attacked by ladybird larvae

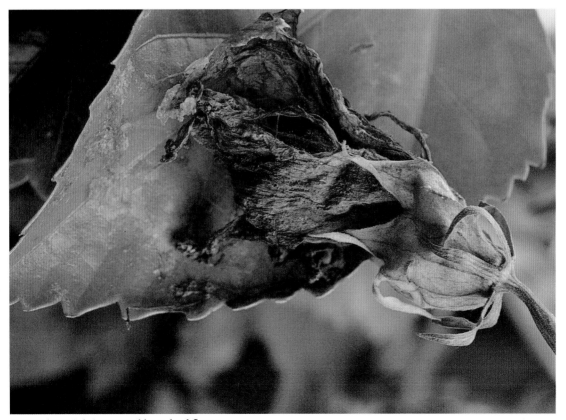

Fungus botrytis being spread by a dead flower

Tomato plant roots afflicted by root knot

Chianapsis scale on an acacia stem

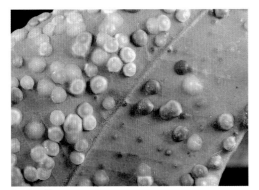

Leaf gall

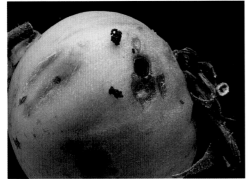

Holes in a tomato caused by the heliothis moth

A golfing green attacked by a fungal disease

Small scale insect colonies can be removed by hand

Beneficial nasturtiums that discourage aphids

Bird netting protecting a peach tree

achieved there is a good chance of it becoming permanent, for female codling moths rarely travel more than 50 metres and males rarely more than two hundred. As long as you stop reinfestation from contaminated boxes and fruit, the chances of large-scale reinfestation should be slight.

Control

You must strike early. If you grow apples, expect the codling moth and make the orchard as unattractive to them as you can. Grow nasturtiums and lavender under the trees. Grow parsnips and let them go to seed all around the orchard so that they are flowering most of the year. You can slash them every now and again so that more flowering stems will spring up. Most importantly, check once a week for holes in the fruit and sawdust deposits on the branches. Remove anything which shows signs of infestation.

Let hens or animals run in the orchard. They will clear up the apples which have fallen because the caterpillars have eaten the seeds and the fruit has rotted, and the caterpillars in the fruit will be unable to pupate. Clear up every other fallen apple and burn it. Do not bury or add to the compost.

Do not make it easy for the caterpillars. Remove all old boxes, ladders and wooden bits and pieces from the orchard, and do not bring in second-hand wood of any sort. Regularly check the corners of sheds for cocoons. Check crab apples and quinces and any apples in storage for any signs of entry of the pest.

Use lure pots to give you an idea of how widespread infection is. The pots themselves will not be all that effective, but they will give you an idea of where and when to spray. To make a lure, fill a glass jar with one part port wine to seven parts water **or** one part molasses to seven parts water. Dribble a little oil on the surface of the water and hang the jars around the orchard, at about shoulder-height and in the warmest spots where the moths are most likely to become active first. Get rid of the drowned insects every morning and renew the lure every week or after a particularly heavy rainstorm.

Other moths may be attracted to the bait. You can recognise the codling moth by its greyish brown colour and the circular, darker shiny area near each wing tip. The moths are about 20 mm from wing to wing.

Spraying

This is only effective against the moth. Once the caterpillar is in the fruit it is relatively unassailable by organic methods. Spray with derris — **but not more than once a fortnight** — underneath, but **not** on top of the leaves, and in any crevice nearby where the moths might be hiding. Spray with a light oil — but only if the temperature is **below** 24^0C — both above and below the leaves. If you use an oil spray in hot weather you will damage the leaves. Spray Dipel directly on to the apples. Dipel is *bacillus thuringiensis* — bacterial warfare against caterpillars. Do this weekly until no more moths are being trapped by the lures. It is less harmful to other inhabitants of the orchard than derris.

Ryania, a plant-derived insecticide, will kill the caterpillars after they have entered the apple. It is reasonably specific against the codling moth caterpillar though it will kill other caterpillars and beetles too. Ryania has had success in the northern hemisphere, but unfortunately it is far less effective in the hotter and harsher conditions of Australia. Try it, if you can get hold of it, but do not expect total success.

Caterpillar control

1. When the caterpillars have finished feeding in the apple, they travel down the tree trunk or along the branches in search of somewhere to pupate. Now is the time to trap them; winter and spring are the most important times but trapping should go on all year round. Scrape away some loose bark from trunk or branch and replace it with a band of old woollen material or corrugated cardboard about 10 cm wide soaked in liquid derris or old sump oil. Inspect every week and renew as necessary.

2. Grease-band trees from the first moth sighting until mid winter so that the caterpillars find it difficult to negotiate the trunks and branches in their search for a place to cocoon.

3. Run animals under the trees.

4. Protect the beneficial predators. Do not use sprays that might harm the birds, spiders, ants, wasps and hoverflies and their larvae which feed on caterpillars. Inspect your apples regularly.

It is possible to control codling moth without resorting to high-residue pesticides, but you need a thorough understanding of moth behaviour and the patience to put in several years of work to continue constant vigilance even after that.

TREES AND SHRUBS

PROBLEMS		
Azalea	Symptoms: Cause: Solution:	Dieback Lime in the soil, roots too hot Never plant in concrete pots; keep soil acid and well mulched.
	Symptoms: Cause: Solution:	Brown patches on leaves Fungal leaf-spot or azalea leaf-miner Spray with garlic which is both a fungicide and insecticide.
	Symptoms: Cause: Solution:	Circular white patches on leaves Powdery mildew Spray with milk, chamomile, chives or casuarina. A baking soda and soap spray may be used in winter. Spray regularly with seaweed, nettle or a general tonic as a preventative.
	Symptoms: Cause: Solution:	White, yellow or gray mottled leaves Azalea lace bug, thrips, white flies, red spider mite Spray with garlic, quassia, wormwood, rhubarb leaf or bug juice. If droppings are evident, spray with pyrethrum every 10 days.
	Symptoms: Cause: Solution:	Pale green, thick swellings with a white patch of spores on leaves in wet weather Leaf gall Cut off and burn affected foliage; spray with casuarina or chive tea when new growth is forming. Use seaweed spray every two weeks as a preventative.

THE ORGANIC GARDEN DOCTOR

PROBLEMS

Azaleas (continued)	Symptoms:	Leaves chewed
	Cause:	Caterpillars
	Solution:	Spray with quassia, garlic or Dipel. *See* **Recipes for pest and disease control**, p.137.
	Symptoms:	Buds and flowers become brown and papery and stay on the bush after unaffected flowers have fallen
	Cause:	Petal blight
	Solution:	Cut off all affected flowers at once. Spray with chamomile, chives or lilac as soon as the flowers start to form — every two days if you have had the problem previously.
Bay	Symptoms:	Lumps on the leaves; lumps on the stems and leaves
	Cause:	White wax scale, pink wax scale
	Solution:	Try a dilute clay spray, then a pyrethrum, garlic or quassia spray if damage is too severe to wait for natural predators. Use an oil spray if temperature is under 24ºC. Grease-band the base of the tree to prevent ants from climbing up.
Beech	Symptoms:	Brown blisters on leaves
	Cause:	Oak blotch miner
	Solution:	Spray with milk. Use an oil spray in cool weather or an azalea spray if all else fails.
Box	Symptoms:	Leaves yellow; twigs die back
	Cause:	Scale
	Solution:	Wait for predators if possible. Interplant with rue, tansy, wormwood or lavender. Grease-band tree to discourage ants. Use a dilute clay spray and if it is not effective use a pyrethrum, garlic or quassia one. Use an oil spray in cool weather.
Camellia	Symptoms:	Failure to flower
	Cause:	Overwatering; underwatering; poor feeding; poor drainage; hot sun on wet buds and flowers
	Solution:	Improve gardening techniques.

PROBLEMS

Camellia (continued)	Symptoms:	Bud drop
	Cause:	Camellia bud mite
	Solution:	Get rid of weeds around bush, particularly clover and capeweed. Spray with milk at any time or oil if temperature is under 24°C.
	Symptoms:	Brown patches on leaves; damaged buds and flowers; fungus on damaged areas
	Cause:	Sunburn
	Solution:	Provide shade
	Symptoms:	Dieback; *Camellia sasanqua* is rarely affected.
	Cause:	*Phytophthora* root-rot
	Solution:	Buy *Camellia japonica* grafted on to *sasanqua* stock.
	Symptoms:	Discoloured leaves
	Cause:	Camellia rust mite
	Solution:	Use milk, coriander, anise or soapy water spray at any time; use an oil spray in cool weather and one of derris as a last resort. Get rid of weeds around the bushes.
	Symptoms:	Dark, corky areas on leaves
	Cause:	Oedemas
	Solution:	Water sparingly in cloudy weather.
	Symptoms:	Small lumps on leaves and stems
	Cause:	Scale
	Solution:	Spray with dilute clay, soapy water, pyrethrum, nicotine or garlic; use an oil spray in cool weather
	Symptoms:	Small insects clustered on stems
	Cause:	Aphids
	Solution:	Jet insects off with water. Spray with nettle and seaweed. Use garlic, onion, lantana, rhubarb leaf spray as a last resort. Grease-band the base of the trunk to deter ants; plant marigolds, lavender or nasturtiums under the bushes.

PROBLEMS		
Camellia (continued)	Symptoms:	Distorted flowers or leaves
	Cause:	Thrips
	Solution:	Some thrips are useful predators and eat mites or aphids. Don't destroy unless they really are badly damaging your plants. Hope for rain or hot dry weather to reduce numbers, encourage wasps, bugs, spiders, fungi, ladybirds, lacewings and other natural controls. Otherwise try strong jets of preferably hot water, dilute clay spray, a soapy water or onion or derris spray.
Cypress	Symptoms:	Branches die back; split bark oozes gum
	Cause:	Canker
	Solution:	Dig out and burn tree.
	Symptoms:	Branches die back; leaves lose colour; larvae chew holes in bark.
	Cause:	Cypress bark weevil or cypress pine beetle
	Solution:	Cut off dead branches. Keep tree growing strongly.
	Symptoms:	Defoliation
	Cause:	Sawflies
	Solution:	*See* **Sawflies**, p.124
Daphne	Symptoms:	Stem rots at ground level
	Cause:	*Sclerotina* rot
	Solution:	Keep mulch away from stem. Cut away affected areas of stem and paint with bordeaux paste.
	Symptoms:	Yellow blotches and irregular streaks on leaves; distorted flowers that fall
	Cause:	Viral disease
	Solution:	Dig out and burn infected plants. Buy virus-resistant cultivars.
Frangipani	Symptoms:	Fleshy stems become hollow with blackened ends
	Cause:	Low temperature; insects invade the damaged area but do not cause the damage.

PROBLEMS		
Frangipani (continued)	Symptoms:	Masses of small scales
	Cause:	Scale
	Solution:	Wait for predators. Spray with milk or dilute clay. Use an oil spray in cool weather and a soap and pyrethrum spray as a last resort.
Fucshia	Symptoms:	Brown patches on upper leaf surface with orange blotches on underside
	Cause:	Rust
	Solution:	Spray with soluble aspirin or willow water. Try chamomile. Spray with bordeaux in winter.
	Symptoms:	Clouds of white flies clustered on shoots and leaves
	Cause:	White flies
	Solution:	Add wood ash, dolomite or rock phosphate to the soil to supply phosphorus and magnesium. Wipe leaves with a soapy kitchen cloth. Use an oil spray in cool conditions under 24°C. Put down yellow boards covered with glue or motor oil to trap the flies. Grow nasturtiums under the bushes.
	Symptoms:	Distorted new shoots
	Cause:	Cyclamen mite
	Solution:	Get rid of weeds around bushes. Spray with milk or oil if temperature is under 24°C. Use derris as a last resort.
	Symptoms:	White, fluffy bulges on stems
	Cause:	Mealy bugs
	Solution:	Dab with methylated spirits. Wipe leaves with soapy kitchen cloth. Grease-band base of the bush to deter ants. Spray with oil if temperature is under 24°C but do not use insecticide — it would be ineffective as it could not penetrate the waxy coating of the mealy bug.
Gardenia	Symptoms:	Burnt flowers
	Cause:	Growing in full sun or dry soil
	Solution:	Plant in a semi-shaded spot and mulch and water regularly.

PROBLEMS		
Gardenia (continued)	Symptoms: Cause: Solution:	Black specks in flowers Thrips Dislodge pests with strong jets of water. Spray with soapy water in the cool of the evening or with onion or derris at any time.
	Symptoms: Cause: Solution:	Scaly encrustations on leaves Scale Wipe leaves with a soapy kitchen cloth. Spray with oil if temperature is under 24°C. Try a pyrethrum, garlic or quassia spray and in bad cases, an azalea spray.
Hawthorn	Symptoms: Cause: Solution:	Skeletonised foliage Pear and cherry slug Dust leaves with flour browned in the oven. Spray with derris, pyrethrum or Dipel. You can ignore the problem — the bush will survive.
Hibiscus	Symptoms: Cause: Solution:	Holes in petals Hibiscus beetles They are pollen feeders; ignore them or just pick them off.
	Symptoms: Cause: Solution:	Yellow flecks on leaves; clear areas on veins Viral disease Dig out and burn the bush.
	Symptoms: Cause: Solution:	Plant pales, wilts and dies; stem rots at ground level Collar-rot Dig out and destroy affected bush. Leave hole open to the weather for three weeks. Do not invite collar-rot by mowing or digging too near stem and damaging it; or by crowding the bush base with other small plants or piling mulch around the stem.

PROBLEMS

Holly	Symptoms:	Pink, brown, black or purple lumps on leaves
	Cause:	Scale
	Solution:	Spray with oil if the temperature is below 24ºC, or with a soapy spray in the cool of the evening. Try derris, quassia or garlic spray as a last resort.
Hydrangea	Symptoms:	Yellow leaves; pale veins
	Cause:	Iron deficiency
	Solution:	Give a regular foliar feed of compost water, green manure or nettle tea until symptoms disappear.
Lilac	Symptoms:	Failure to flower
	Cause:	Lilac takes several years to establish itself enough to flower.
	Symptoms:	Large black spots on leaves
	Cause:	Bacterial leaf spot
	Solution:	Spray with bordeaux in winter and with chamomile, casuarina or lilac in summer. Spraying regularly with seaweed or a tonic spray will help to prevent leaf spot.
Maple	Symptoms:	Cracked bark
	Cause:	Longicorn beetle larvae
	Solution:	Inspect regularly and plug up holes with grafting wax. Encourage birds into the garden.
Monterey pine *(Pinus radiata)*	Symptoms:	Holes in bark; sawdust deposits
	Cause:	Sirex wasp which attacks poorly growing trees or trees growing where the rainfall is low and erratic
	Solution:	Keep trees well fed and watered.
Oleander	Symptoms:	Scaly spots on leaves
	Cause:	Oleander and other scales
	Solution:	Spray with oil if the temperature is under 24ºC; spray with soapy water in the cool of the evening. Pyrethrum, garlic or quassia spray can be used as a last resort.

PROBLEMS		
Oleander (continued)	Symptoms: Cause: Solution:	Chewed leaves Oleander butterfly caterpillars Dust leaves with white pepper. Spray with garlic, derris, quassia or Dipel. Encourage birds and other predators.
Poplar	Symptoms: Cause: Solution:	Brown patches on leaves Anthracnose Improve air circulation and drainage around tree. Cut off and burn all affected foliage. Spray with bordeaux in cool weather.
	Symptoms: Cause: Solution:	Brown-edged leaves Salt in the water Use rainwater if tap water is salty.
	Symptoms: Cause: Solution:	Yellow flecked leaves, premature leaf-drop Rust Keep tree growing as strongly as possible. Spray regularly with seaweed or another plant tonic. In a bad case, dig out tree and replace with a rust-resistant variety.
Rhododendron		*See* Azalea
Umbrella tree	Symptoms: Cause: Solution:	Blackened or sticky leaves Mealy bugs Use an oil spray if temperature is below 24⁰C or a soapy water spray in the cool of the evening. Other insecticides are a waste of time. Grease-band the base of the tree to deter ants.
	Symptoms: Cause: Solution:	Black, brown or pink scaly patches on leaves and stems Scale Use an oil spray if the temperature is under 24⁰C; use soapy water spray in the cool of the evening. Try a dilute clay, pyrethrum, quassia or garlic spray. *See* **Recipes for pest and disease control, p.137.**

PROBLEMS		
Viburnum	Symptoms:	Dull, mottled leaves
	Cause:	Thrips
	Solution:	Blast pests off with strong jets of water. Use soapy water spray in the cool of the evening and onion or derris spray at any time. Hope for rainy or hot weather.
	Symptoms:	White scaly patches on leaves
	Cause:	White palm scale
	Solution:	Use an oil spray when temperature is under 24ºC; soapy water spray in the cool of the evening and dilute clay, garlic or pyrethrum spray at any time.
White cedar	Symptoms:	Defoliation
	Cause:	Caterpillars
	Solution:	Use quassia, garlic, pyrethrum or Dipel spray. *See* **Codling moth**, pp.88-90. Encourage bird and wasp predators.
Willow	Symptoms:	Pale yellow flecks on leaves
	Cause:	Rust
	Solution:	Spray with chamomile. Use bordeaux when the tree is dormant.
	Symptoms:	Pale green or reddish lumps on leaves
	Cause:	Willow sawfly
	Solution:	Though the galls are ugly, they do not harm the tree. *See* **Sawflies**, p.124

Root-rots

When foliage wilts, the tree begins to die back, suddenly or gradually, and is wobbly in the ground, you have root-rot. *Phytophthora cinammoni* affects both trees and plants. Large roots become brittle, small roots die. *Amarillaria* rot is detectable when small yellow toadstools grow around a tree and, on inspection, a white fungal sheath is found to be growing over the roots.

You must be vigilant against root-rots. Do not allow them in. Beware of muddy boots, infected water, earth-moving equipment and bought nursery stock. Keep up the level of organic matter in the soil but do not dig in undecomposed organic matter; let it rot first. Good compost will inhibit root-rots. Add dolomite to the soil to raise the pH level; use blood and bone as high-phosphorus fertiliser to keep the trees and plants growing strongly. Make sure drainage is good. If you cannot, plant trees in a sloping mound on top of the soil; do not dig them in. Do not go in for sudden bursts of overhead watering. Do not use artificial, high-nitrogen fertilisers. Encourage microflora in the soil by keeping it moist and allowing the build-up of organic matter. Do not dig around trees.

Cut back infected trees so that the damaged roots have less to support. Give a nourishing foliar spray of seaweed or compost water once a week while the tree is recuperating. Mulch with good compost, lucerne hay or wilted comfrey so that the micro-organisms in the soil can get the rot under control and allow the roots to re-establish.

If there is no hope and trees have to be dug out, remove *all* the roots and burn them. Dig well beyond the drip line to make certain you have found them all. Leave the hole in the ground open to the weather for at least six months before considering planting anything else there. A large fire on the site might be an added protective measure.

If only one tree is affected and the water from it runs downhill and so could affect other trees, dig it out at once before the infection can spread. You can prevent armillaria rot by making sure there are no old tree roots left in the ground you propose to plant. If you fail, dig away the soil for about 60 cm around the tree and expose the roots to the sunlight. Cut out any that are affected. Fill the hole with fresh soil when the infection has cleared. Do not use mulch or compost, or water may pool in the hole. Feed the tree well until it picks up.

Lichen

Lichen are a symbiotic association of fungi and algae that can be green, grey, scaly, bushy, soft, hard or stringy. They are more likely to bother you than the tree. However, if they appear to cover the tree you could scrub them off or paint them with bordeaux paste. If you spray evergreens with bordeaux in winter you will have to avoid leaves and flowers.

The Organic Growers Association of Western Australia recommends using 100 grams of skimmed milk to every two kilos of copper sulphate to make a more effective bordeaux mixture. *See* **Recipes for pest and disease control.**

Sooty Mould

Sooty mould can attack most ornamentals and make them look as though they have been dusted with soot. The problem is mainly aesthetic but, if it persists, can affect photosynthesis and the vigour of the plant. The mould grows on the sugary secretions of aphids, mealy bugs and scale; eliminate these pests and the mould will peel off during the next few months. Once pests have been controlled, hose the plant vigorously with hot water if possible to clean it, or use a damp kitchen cloth for leaves within reach.

FLOWERS

PROBLEMS		
Ageratum	Symptoms: Cause: Solution:	Distorted leaves; small green insects on foliage Aphids Grow wormwood, tansy, marigolds or lavender nearby as a deterrent. Spray with dilute Vegemite to attract natural predators. Put reflective foil on the soil around the plants. Wait three weeks for natural predators to build up before spraying dilute clay, nettle, wormwood or seaweed. As a last resort, use a derris, rhubarb leaf or garlic spray. In cold weather use a baking soda spray.
Ajuga	Symptoms: Cause: Solution:	Grey film on the leaves Powdery mildew Spray with milk, chamomile, chives, elder, casuarina, horsetail or double strength garlic. Use washing soda or Condy's crystals to make a spray in cold weather.
Alyssum	Symptoms: Cause: Solution:	Plant droops, stem rots at ground level Stem-rot Dig out and burn all infected plants and leave the holes exposed to the weather for three weeks. Remove dead foliage at the bottom of healthy plants to improve air drainage and water with chamomile or chive tea. *See* **Recipes for pest and disease control, p.137**
Anemone	Symptoms: Cause: Solution:	Distorted leaves; small green insects on plant Aphids Grow wormwood, tansy, marigolds or lavender nearby as a deterrent. Spray with dilute Vegemite to attract natural predators. Put reflective foil on the soil around the plants. Wait three weeks for natural predators to build up before spraying dilute clay, nettle, wormwood or seaweed. As a last resort, use a derris, rhubarb leaf or garlic spray. In cold weather use a baking soda spray.

PROBLEMS		
Aster	Symptoms:	Grey film on leaves
	Cause:	Powdery mildew
	Solution:	Spray with milk, chamomile, chives, elder, casuarina, horsetail or double strength garlic. Use washing soda or Condy's crystals to make a spray in cold weather.
	Symptoms:	Centre leaves distorted
	Cause:	Aster grub
	Solution:	Cut out affected part; spray with derris or Dipel.
	Symptoms:	Dull, pitted foliage
	Cause:	Red spider mites
	Solution:	Remove and burn affected foliage. Overhead water in hot dry weather. Do not use pesticides, even organic ones, to allow the beneficial predators — thrips, ladybirds and lacewing larvae — to build-up and clear the pests for you. Use an oil spray if the temperature is under 20°C, or soapy water spray if it is under 24°C, anise or coriander sprays at any time and derris or quassia sprays as a last resort.
Astilbe	Symptoms:	Brown leaf margins
	Solution:	Water thoroughly and regularly. If the soil is deficient in potash mulch with comfrey or add some woodash.
Bedding begonia	Symptoms:	Brown-edged leaves
	Cause:	Brown vegetable weevil
	Solution:	Spray with pyrethrum or derris.
Bellis perennis	Symptoms:	Raised orange dots on leaves
	Cause:	Rust
	Solution:	Spray with soluble aspirin, willow-water or chamomile tea. Bordeaux can be used in cool weather.

PROBLEMS		
Brachycombe (Swan River daisy)	Symptoms: Cause: Solution:	Curled or distorted leaves Aphids Grow wormwood, tansy, marigolds or lavender nearby as a deterrent. Spray with Vegemite dissolved in water to attract natural predators. Put down reflective foil on the soil around the plants. Wait three weeks for natural predators to build up before spraying with either dilute clay, nettle, wormwood or seaweed. As a last resort, use a derris, rhubarb leaf or garlic spray. In cold weather use a baking soda spray.
Calendula	Symptoms: Cause: Solution:	Large rusty circles on leaves or stems Rust Spray with bordeaux in cool weather. Try a strong spray of chamomile, soluble aspirin or willow water.
Canterbury bells	Symptoms: Cause: Solution:	Older leaves curl at the edges; small green insects cluster on new shoots Aphids Grow wormwood, tansy, marigolds or lavender nearby as a deterrent. Spray with Vegemite dissolved in water to attract natural predators. Put down reflective foil on the soil around the plants. Wait three weeks for natural predators to build up before spraying with either dilute clay, nettle, wormwood or seaweed. As a last resort, use a derris, rhubarb leaf or garlic spray. In cold weather use a baking soda spray.
	Symptoms: Cause: Solution:	Dull, 'sand-blasted' leaves Red spider mites Remove and burn affected foliage. Overhead water in hot dry weather. Do not use pesticides, even organic ones, to allow the beneficial predators — thrips, ladybirds and lacewing larvae — to build-up and clear the pests for you. Use an oil spray if the temperature is under 20ºC, or soapy water spray if it is under 24ºC, anise or coriander sprays at any time and derris or quassia sprays as a last resort.

PROBLEMS		
Canterbury bells (continued)	Symptoms: Cause: Solution:	Grey film on leaves Powdery mildew Spray with milk, chamomile, chives, elder, casuarina, horsetail or double strength garlic. Use washing soda or Condy's crystals to make a spray in cold weather.
Carnations	Symptoms: Cause: Solution:	Rusty spots on leaves Rust Spray with chamomile tea, soluble aspirin or willow-water. Spray soil around plants with bordeaux in winter.
	Symptoms: Cause: Solution:	Dark spots on leaves Mildew or leaf-spot Use seaweed spray as a preventative. Spray infected plants with milk, chives, elder, double strength garlic or horsetail tea. Spray with washing soda in cool weather.
	Symptoms: Cause: Solution:	Streaked flowers Thrips Dislodge them from the plants with strong jets of water. They eat mites and aphids, so do not destroy them unless they are really damaging the plants. Encourage wasps, bugs, spiders, fungi, ladybirds, lacewings — the natural controllers — and hope for rain or hot dry weather to reduce the thrip population. Sprays made from dilute clay, soapy water, onion or derris are effective against them.
Cheiranthus (Perennial wallflower)	Symptoms: Cause: Solution:	Skeletonised tracery on leaves Leaf-miner Spray with soapy water, pyrethrum, rhubarb leaf or bug juice.
Chrysanthemum	Symptoms: Cause: Solution:	Brown sunken patches in flower buds; pale tracery on leaves Bud grub Spray with dilute clay, pyrethrum, rhubarb leaf or elder at any time; use oil if the temperature is under 20°C and soapy water if it is under 24°C.

PROBLEMS

Chrysanthemum (continued)	Symptoms:	Distorted leaves; small black or brown insects clustered below flower buds or on new shoots
	Cause:	Black aphids
	Solution:	Grow wormwood, tansy, marigolds or lavender nearby as a deterrent. Spray with Vegemite dissolved in water to attract natural predators. Put down reflective foil on the soil around the plants. Wait three weeks for natural predators to build up before spraying with either dilute clay, nettle, wormwood or seaweed. As a last resort use a derris, rhubarb leaf or garlic spray. In cold weather use a baking soda spray.
	Symptoms:	Shrivelled, blackened foliage
	Cause:	Leaf eelworm
	Solution:	Saturate soil around the infected plants with pyrethrum spray or a one-in-ten molasses solution. Increase humus level of the soil; add compost. Mulch well, particularly if soil is sandy.
Cineraria	Symptoms:	Grey tracery on leaves
	Cause:	Leaf-miner
	Solution:	Spray with soapy water, pyrethrum, rhubarb leaf spray or bug juice.
Cornflower	Symptoms:	Stunted or deformed leaves or flowers
	Cause:	Aphids
	Solution:	Spray with dilute clay and use nettle or wormwood as a last resort. Interplant with lavender, tansy or wormwood.
Dahlia	Symptoms:	Dull, pitted foliage
	Cause:	Red spider mites
	Solution:	Remove and burn affected foliage. Overhead water in hot dry weather. Do not use pesticides, even organic ones, to allow the beneficial predators — thrips, ladybirds and lacewing larvae — to build-up and clear the pests for you. Use an oil spray if the temperature is under 20°C, or soapy water spray if it is under 24°C, anise or coriander sprays at any time and derris or quassia sprays as a last resort.

PROBLEMS		
Dahlia (continued)	Symptoms: Cause: Solution:	Failure to flower Incorrect feeding; too much nitrogen Mulch soil around plants with woodchips and a handful of ground rock phosphate.
	Symptoms: Cause: Solution:	Flowers have blackened edges; tiny black insects on plant Thrips Some thrips are useful predators and eat mites or aphids. Don't destroy unless they are really damaging your plants. Hope for rain or hot dry weather to reduce numbers; encourage wasps, bugs, spiders, fungi, ladybirds, lacewings and other natural controls. Otherwise try strong jets of preferably hot water, dilute clay spray, a soapy water spray, onion or derris spray.
	Symptoms: Cause: Solution:	Flowers and foliage eaten Slugs and snails *See* **Slugs and snails**, p.28.
Delphinium	Symptoms: Cause: Solution:	Grey film on foliage Powdery mildew Spray with milk, chamomile, chives, elder, casuarina, horsetail or double strength garlic. Use washing soda or Condy's crystals to make a spray in cold weather.
	Symptoms: Cause: Solution:	Plant wilts suddenly; stem rots at ground level Crown-rot Cut out and burn all infected plants and leave the holes in the soil open to the weather for three weeks. Cut away low growth around remaining plants to increase air flow around them.
Foxglove	Symptoms: Cause: Solution:	Red flecks on leaves Rust Cut off affected leaves. Spray with chamomile, soluble aspirin or willow-water. You can use bordeaux at half strength but there is a risk of damaging flowers and buds. *See* **Recipes for pest and disease control**, p.137

PROBLEMS

Foxglove (continued)	Symptoms:	Dull, brownish leaves
	Cause:	Red spider mites
	Solution:	Remove and burn affected foliage. Overhead water in hot dry weather. Do not use pesticides, even organic ones, to allow the beneficial predators — thrips, ladybirds and lacewing larvae — to build-up and clear the pests for you. Use an oil spray if the temperature is under 20°C, or soapy water spray if it is under 24°C, anise or coriander sprays at any time and derris or quassia sprays as a last resort.
Geraniums	Symptoms:	Yellow spots on top of leaves; corresponding brown spots on the underside
	Cause:	Rust
	Solution:	Cut off affected leaves. Spray with chamomile, soluble aspirin or willow-water.
	Symptoms:	Plant wilts suddenly, stem rots at ground level
	Cause:	Stem-rot
	Solution:	Dig out infected plants or cut out parts of the plant and remove the soil immediately around them. Drench the remaining soil with chamomile tea. Use the healthy tips of the infected stems as cuttings.
	Symptoms:	Holes in the leaves
	Cause:	Caterpillars
	Solution:	Pick off caterpillars by hand. Spray with derris, Dipel or white pepper.
	Symptoms:	Flowers rot in wet weather
	Cause:	Botrytis rot
	Solution:	Cut off affected flowers; spray plants with chamomile, casuarina, elder or lilac.
Gerbera	Symptoms:	Rotted flower centres
	Cause:	Bud grub
	Solution:	Spray with pyrethrum, rhubarb leaf, white pepper, derris or Dipel.

PROBLEMS		
Gerbera (continued)	Symptoms:	Deformed flowers and stems
	Cause:	Aphids
	Solution:	Grow wormwood, tansy, marigolds or lavender nearby as a deterrent. Spray with Vegemite dissolved in water to attract natural predators. Put down reflective foil on the soil around the plants. Wait three weeks for natural predators to build up before spraying with either dilute clay, nettle, wormwood or seaweed. As a last resort, use a derris, rhubarb leaf or garlic spray. In cold weather use a baking soda spray.
	Symptoms:	Green flowers
	Cause:	Viral disease
	Solution:	Dig out infected plants and burn. Control the aphids which carry the virus.
	Symptoms:	Raised white flecks on leaves and stems
	Cause:	White rust
	Solution:	Pick off infected leaves and stems. Spray with bordeaux, but only when the air is cool. Try a spray of chamomile or double strength garlic.
Hollyhocks	Symptoms:	Rusty spots on leaves
	Cause:	Rust
	Solution:	Spray with half strength bordeaux in cool weather. Otherwise use a double strength chamomile or soluble aspirin spray.
	Symptoms:	Holes in leaves
	Cause:	Slugs and snails; caterpillars
	Cause:	See **Slugs and snails**, p.28. Spray leaves with derris or Dipel for caterpillars.
Larkspur	Symptoms:	Grey film on leaves; yellowing foliage
	Cause:	Mildew
	Solution:	Cut off affected leaves and flowers. Spray with either elder, chives, lilac or double strength garlic or chamomile.

PROBLEMS		
Larkspur (continued)	Symptoms:	Dull, possibly yellowing foliage; tiny insects just visible to the naked eye
	Cause:	Red spider mites
	Solution:	Remove and burn affected foliage. Overhead water in hot dry weather. Do not use pesticides, even organic ones, to allow the beneficial predators — thrips, ladybirds and lacewing larvae — to build-up and clear the pests for you. Use an oil spray if the temperature is under 20ºC, or soapy water spray if it is under 24ºC, anise or coriander sprays at any time and derris or quassia sprays as a last resort.
Lavender	Symptoms:	Foliage near ground becomes brown on the underside.
	Cause:	Mildew
	Solution:	Cut out affected foliage to improve air and light circulation around the plant. Replace old plants with young ones. Spray with chives, elder or double strength chamomile tea. Use a half strength bordeaux spray in winter.
Lobelia	Symptoms:	Dull cream mottling on leaves
	Cause:	Jassid leaf-hopper
	Solution:	Spray with oil or soapy water in cool weather or with pyrethrum or derris at any time.
Marigolds	Symptoms:	Dull, 'sand-blasted' foliage
	Cause:	Red spider mites
	Solution:	Remove adjacent weeds and all affected foliage. Spray with soapy water, anise or coriander. Use derris if these fail.
	Symptoms:	Greenish spots on upper side of leaf, orange ones on the underside
	Cause:	Rust
	Solution:	Remove infected plants at once and burn. Clean up any debris left from a previous crop of marigolds. If there have been previous rust problems keep the marigolds away from other flowers and weeds. Spray with soluble aspirin or willow-water.

PROBLEMS		
Mesembry-anthemum	Symptoms: Cause: Solution:	Yellow spots on leaves which subsequently shrivel Rust Remove affected leaves at once. Spray with soluble aspirin or willow-water. Use bordeaux only if you are certain you can keep the spray away from flowers and buds.
Nasturtium	Symptoms: Cause: Solution:	Fine tracery eaten out of leaves Leaf-miner Spray with pyrethrum or garlic at any time and with oil or soapy water in cool weather.
Paeony rose	Symptoms: Cause: Solution:	Slimy petals, waterlogged spots on flowers; small reddish spots that turn large and brown on leaves; stems may rot Botrytis leaf and flower spot Remove all diseased and spent flowers and burn them. Spray plant with chamomile, elder, casuarina or double strength garlic. *See* **Recipes for pest and disease control, p.137**
	Symptoms: Cause:	Failure to flower Spring may have been too hot and short; paeonies need several years to establish themselves strongly enough to flower.
	Symptoms: Solution:	Rotten buds and leaves Improve air drainage around the plant and keep mulch away from them while they are flowering.
Pansy	Symptoms: Cause: Solution:	Distorted leaves; small insects on plants Aphids Spray with pyrethrum, wormwood or garlic. Use a baking soda spray in cool weather.
Perennial phlox	Symptoms: Cause: Solution:	Green flowers Viral disease Remove and burn infected plants without delay. Use a seaweed spray as a preventative.

PROBLEMS		
Phlox drummondii	Symptoms:	White or transparent leaves; scanty flowers
	Cause:	Unwise feeding; too much nitrogen
	Solution:	Mulch the ground around the plants with wood-chips or oat-hay. Do not feed.
Polyanthus	Symptoms:	Plants wilt; growth is stunted; tiny downy white insects appear on leaves and roots
	Cause:	Mealy bugs
	Solution:	Plant wormwood or tansy nearby to repel the ants which contribute to the trouble. Encourage the natural predators — ladybirds, lacewing larvae and parasitic chalcid wasps. Prune off all infected foliage. Mealy bugs have a protective coating insecticide sprays cannot penetrate — you might try an oil spray in cool weather or a soapy water spray at night. Do not replant plants of the same family in soil where the mealy bugs have been troublesome.
Portulacca	Symptoms:	Plant wilts and dies
	Cause:	Overwatering and undecomposed organic matter in the soil
Poppy	Symptoms:	Twisted stems
	Cause:	Wind damage
	Solution:	Mulch around the plant thickly.
	Symptoms:	Enlarged buds that fail to open; yellow-lined plants
	Cause:	Viral disease
	Solution:	Burn all infected plants without delay.
	Symptoms:	White film over leaves
	Cause:	Mildew
	Solution:	Spray with milk, chamomile, chives, elder, casuarina, horsetail or double strength garlic. Use washing soda or Condy's crystals to make a spray in cold weather.
Ranunculus	Symptoms:	Twisted stems; clusters of tiny insects
	Cause:	Aphids
	Solution:	Spray with wormwood, garlic or rhubarb leaf.

PROBLEMS		
Ranunculus (continued)	Symptoms:	Brown or transparent circles on leaves
	Cause:	Shot-hole
	Solution:	Spray with bordeaux in winter and with chamomile, chive, elder or casuarina at any time.
	Symptoms:	Seedlings die suddenly; stems and leaves rot
	Cause:	Seedling blight
	Solution:	Never plant seedlings in sodden ground, always make sure it is well drained. Pull out and destroy affected seedlings and drench the rest in chamomile tea.
Stock	Symptoms:	Streaked flowers
	Cause:	Viral disease
	Solution:	Dig out and burn affected plants. Control the aphids which carry the virus.
	Symptoms:	Brown, wilted leaves and blackened stems
	Cause:	Bacterial rot
	Solution:	Make sure infected plants do not seed.
Sweet peas	Symptoms:	Plants suddenly wilt and die
	Cause:	Root and stem fungi
	Solution:	Remove affected plants and burn them. Do not plant sweet peas near broad beans.
	Symptoms:	Failure to flower
	Cause:	Excessive temperature, hot or cold
	Symptoms:	Grey film over leaves
	Cause:	Mildew
	Solution:	Pick off affected leaves. Spray plant with garlic, elder or chamomile.
Verbena	Symptoms:	Pale film over leaves
	Cause:	Mildew
	Solution:	Pick off affected leaves. Spray plant with garlic, elder or chamomile.

PROBLEMS			
Violet	Symptoms:		Fine, yellow mottling on leaves
	Cause:		Red spider mites
	Solution:		Water well in spring and summer. Remove and burn affected foliage. Overhead water in hot dry weather. Do not use pesticides, even organic ones, to allow the beneficial predators — thrips, ladybirds and lacewing larvae — to build-up and clear the pests for you. Use an oil spray if the temperature is under 20⁰C, or soapy water spray if it is under 24⁰C, anise or coriander sprays at any time and derris or quassia sprays as a last resort.
	Symptoms:		Small, water-soaked spots on leaves; they enlarge to grey-brown, scabby patches; dead material in the centre may fall out and leave a hole
	Cause:		Violet scab
	Solution:		Remove and burn infected part of the plant. Spray with elder, casuarina, chamomile or double strength garlic. *See* **Recipes for pest and disease control**, p.137
Wallflower	Symptoms:		Pale, skeletonised areas in leaves
	Cause:		Leaf-miner
	Solution:		Spray with garlic or pyrethrum at any time, or soapy water in cool weather or late evening.
Zinnia	Symptoms:		Tunnels in flowers
	Cause:		Flower grub
	Solution:		Spray with pyrethrum, derris or Dipel. *See* **Recipes for pest and disease control**, p.137
	Symptoms:		Plants wilt and darken
	Cause:		Fusarium wilt
	Solution:		Pull up and burn affected plants. Drench the ground with casuarina tea and keep covered with clear plastic for three weeks before replanting in it.
	Symptoms:		Grey film on leaves
	Cause:		Powdery mildew
	Solution:		Pick off affected leaves. Spray with chamomile, chives, elder or lilac.

ROSES

PESTS		
Leaf pests	Symptoms:	Reddish brown patches on the surface of the leaves and webbing on the underside; leaves become mottled and fall.
	Cause:	Red spider mites or two-spotted mite.
	Solution:	Cover nearby weeds with a thick mulch. Remove and burn all infected foliage. Overhead water in dry weather. Thrips, mites, lacewing larvae and a small ladybird are natural predators. You can buy predacious mites — study gardening magazines for advertisements. Milk, onion, garlic, derris and quasia sprays are effective. Use an oil only if temperature is under 24°C.
	Symptoms:	Irregular pieces chewed out of leaves
	Cause:	Caterpillars
	Solution:	Pick off caterpillars or their cocoons by hand. Dust leaves with pepper or ground rock phosphate. Spray with Dipel. Encourage birds.
	Symptoms:	Round or oval pieces chewed out of the leaves
	Cause:	Leaf-cutting bees
	Solution:	These bees rarely cause much damage.
Flower pests	Symptoms:	Blackened petal edges, mottled or deformed flowers
	Cause:	Thrips
	Solution:	Jet them off the plants with hot water or use a soap, onion or derris spray. Encourage their natural predators — wasps, fungi, ladybirds, spiders and lacewings. Watch out for them in hot, thundery weather.

PESTS		
Stem pests	Symptoms:	Tiny, overlapping grey to white scales on the stems
	Cause:	Scale
	Solution:	Squash small groups with your fingers and leave them on the plants to attract predators, or wipe them off with a damp kitchen cloth, or dab them with cotton wool dipped in methylated spirits. As a last resort use garlic, soap, pyrethrum, nicotine or quassia spray, or an oil spray if the temperature is under 24°C. If the scale is cottony it will not do much damage other than to spread sooty mould. Use the controls outlined above and encourage ladybirds which are voracious scale predators.
	Symptoms:	Tiny green, orange, red or brown insects clustered on new growth
	Cause:	Aphids
	Solution:	If spring aphids are a recurring problem plant flowers that bloom in late winter to early spring to attract hoverflies, ladybirds, birds and wasps to your garden so that they are there when the aphids arrive. Plant lavender, particularly cotton lavender, chives or marigolds under the rose bushes. Once they are growing well do not give the roses any nitrogenous fertiliser; use mulch and compost. If you find aphids on the roses wait for three weeks to see if the natural predators will clear them up; if they do not, jet the pests off the plants with strong jets of water. You can use sprays made from nettles, seaweed, garlic, rhubarb leaf and derris dust, but these poisons should not be necessary.
	Symptoms:	Furry or knobby growths on the stems
	Cause:	Gall wasps
	Solution:	They do not cause much harm, but pull them off if you find them unsightly.
Root pests	Symptoms:	Unhealthy-looking bush; wobbly in the ground
	Cause:	Ants
	Solution:	Find the nest under the bush and pour boiling water or pyrethrum and water into it. If you grow tansy around the bushes you will deter ants. Grease-bands will prevent them climbing up into the bush.

PESTS

Root pests (continued)	Symptoms:	Stunted, slow-growing bushes with pale green leaves
	Cause:	Eelworms (nematodes)
	Solution:	Soak the ground below the bushes with a solution of molasses or sugar and water. Add humus to the soil. Grow marigolds near the bushes and chop them into the ground in winter. Prevention is the best long-term solution as, once nematodes get in, they are hard to get out. Before planting a new rose bush hold the soil-free roots in water at 46°C for 16 minutes. This will kill any larvae in the roots.

DISEASES

	Symptoms:	Dead dark wood, split stem. If the canker circles the whole stem, all the growth above it will be affected.
	Cause:	Canker
	Solution:	Keep pruning wounds as small as possible. Dip secateurs in methylated spirits after use. Deal with water trickling down the stem and being trapped between branches. Cut dead wood back to healthy tissue and paint wound with bordeaux paste. Keep bushes growing strongly until the wound heals.
	Symptoms:	Rusty orange specks on the back of leaves, especially in spring. The upper side of the leaves may have a corresponding light patch; leaves may eventually fall
	Cause:	Rust
	Solution:	Plant rust-resistant varieties. Spray with a green manure spray to supply needed potash — a mixture of comfrey leaves and seaweed is excellent. Make regular use of compost, lucerne or comfrey mulch to keep up the supply of potash in the soil.
	Symptoms:	Shoots die from the tips downward
	Cause:	Dieback
	Solution:	Canker, black spot, waterlogging, frost or mineral deficiency can all cause dieback so try to pinpoint which it is. Cut off all affected shoots. If there is no obvious reason, spray as for black spot.

DISEASES

	Symptoms:	Black spots on the leaves or yellow and black splodges; leaves fall in severe cases
	Cause:	Black spot
	Solution:	Make sure there is free air circulation around the bushes. Do not plant tall flowers underneath them; keep the ground cover as low as possible. Chamomile and garlic *may* enable the rose to resist black spot. Keep overhead watering to a minimum. Mulch well in summer; put the hose under the mulch so that leaves and stems do not get wet and spores do not splash up on to the foliage. Remove and burn all affected leaves and prunings. Old-fashioned roses seem particularly susceptible to black spot — La Reine Victoria and Mme Pierre Olger especially. You will either have to supply them with an umbrella each or replace them. Try horsetail, seaweed, casuarina, milk or lilac spray, at fortnightly intervals to prevent black spot forming or stop it spreading. Chamomile or chive tea are milder but can be effective. Spray the dormant bushes with bordeaux. Once is enough for mild cases; for more severe ones spray at leaf-fall, midwinter and just before the buds swell.
	Symptoms:	White or grey powder on leaves and stalks; leaves drop prematurely
	Cause:	Powdery mildew
	Solution:	Improve air circulation around bushes. Mildew strikes when leaves are damp but the roots are dry so watch out in humid weather when it has not rained for some time. Do not use sprinklers or any overhead method of watering. Water under the mulch around the bushes, do not plant roses near fishponds or allow any puddles in their vicinity. Do not grow tall flowers under the bushes. Pick off affected leaves at once and burn. Be careful not to transfer spores from one bush to another on gardening gloves. Regular spraying with horsetail, seaweed or casuarina tea will help to prevent the mildew from developing; chamomile or chive tea should be sprayed on affected bushes and, in bad cases, bordeaux spray used in winter will help.

DISEASES

	Symptoms:	Leaves yellow, shoots and twigs die.
	Cause:	Root-rot, honey fungus or armillaria rot. If toadstools grow next to a bush in autumn or winter or after a cool, wet spell, you have armillaria rot.
	Solution:	Do not use a sawdust mulch near the bushes — it will encourage the fungi. If you must use sawdust, compost it first. Compost inhibits many pathogens. Mulch with good-quality mulch repeatedly and do not dig the soil. Well-mulched or composted plants can survive even if infected; the good feeling makes up for the root damage. Dig out badly infected bushes with as much soil as possible and leave the hole open to the weather for at least two months before you reuse the soil in that position. Keeping an affected area covered with clear plastic for six weeks should kill off the pathogens in the soil.
	Symptoms:	Mosaic patterns on leaves and irregular blemishes on petals
	Cause:	Viruses
	Solution:	You can neither prevent nor control viral diseases. Fortunately, they suppress growth only slightly and are not easily passed on, so you may as well ignore the symptoms. In future buy roses only from a reputable nursery.

OTHER ROSE PROBLEMS

	Symptoms:	Dull, yellow, drooping leaves with brown edges; white encrustations on soil around the bush
	Cause:	Excessive salt or chlorine in the water
	Solution:	Do not use water from chlorinated swimming pools, or artificial fertilisers high in murate of potash.
	Symptoms:	Yellow or bleached patches on leaves; possible withering or browning
	Cause:	Too much sun and too little water
	Solution:	Protect bush with shade-cloth. Mulch the soil to cool it and water regularly.

OTHER ROSE PROBLEMS

	Symptoms: Cause: Solution:	Dull, lifeless leaves The bush may be planted too deeply Dig down to root level and cover the roots with compost or a light leaf-litter. Slope the ground level away from the bush.
	Symptoms: Cause: Solution:	Drooping, pale leaves which have lost their shine Soil may be too acid or too alkaline. Correct the pH of the soil. If it is too alkaline use a mulch of pine needles or peat moss; if it is too acid add wood ash, lime, dolomite or well-made compost. Roses in over-acid or over-alkaline soil could be starving to death because the nutrients in the soil are not available to them. Mulch well. Do not dig or use harsh fertilisers, herbicides or soil sterilants.
	Symptoms: Cause: Solution:	Flower petals browning Exposure to sun and wind Protect the bushes with shade-cloth or a screen of taller plants.
	Symptoms: Solution:	Leaves look as though they have been burned; leaves fall Check to see if your neighbour has been using an organo-phosphate spray.
	Symptoms: Cause: Solution:	Blind shoots It may be an inherent fault in the variety, or the flower bud may have been damaged. If a new shoot loses its flexible sappiness, cut it back halfway to just above an outward-facing bud.
	Symptoms: Cause: Solution:	Small stunted bushes; yellowed leaves with burned edges; small blooms that do not last Check to see if the bush is waterlogged. If it is, the roots are rotting and the bush is starving to death. Dig a drain at least 40 cm deep and certainly as deep as the rose roots on ground *above* the bush and divert water away from it. Foliar feed as a temporary measure while the bush is recovering. If you do not feel like taking this amount of trouble, dig the bush out and resite.

OTHER ROSE PROBLEMS

	Symptoms:	Blackened shoots and brown twigs
	Cause:	Frost damage or unwise pruning
	Solution:	Roses pruned at the beginning of winter when the wood is still sappy can be severely damaged, if not killed, by frost. Do not prune too hard too early. Repeated hard pruning of some floribundas, or any rose in poor condition, can lead to dieback.
	Symptoms:	Twisted leaves and stalks, black or reddish stems
	Cause:	Damage from herbicides
	Solution:	Do not use weed-killers in the garden. If you absolutely must, do not do it on a windy day. Cut off the affected parts of the bush and water well, making certain you are not watering more herbicide into the soil.
	Symptoms:	Rose bushes sicken when planted where rose bushes grew before
	Cause:	The exact cause is not known but it probably has to do with a mineral deficiency and a pathogen build-up to which the roses formerly growing there had managed to adapt.
	Solution:	Dig the bush out and replace as much soil as possible with compost and some good active soil before replanting the bush.

Sunflowers are excellent green manure if used before flowering

Pumpkins growing freely in an open grassy area

Grown together, flowers and fruit discourage pests and encourage predators

Caterpillar infested cabbages

Mulched strawberries

Mulch left on top of the soil will not cause onion rot

Cauliflowers suffering from molybdenum deficiency

Watermelons grown on mulch

Mulched silver beet seedlings

Potato plants infested by aphids

Inflated wine cask bladders used to scare birds

Young mulched citrus trees

BULBS, CORMS AND RHIZOMES

General care

1. Make sure any organic matter in the soil near the growing bulbs is well rotted.
2. Do not overfeed. A thin scattering of blood and bone once a year after flowering is all that is necessary. Over-fed bushes become soft and disease-prone.
3. Do not dig around bulbs. Any damage will cause them to rot.
4. Make sure the soil is well drained — lightly moist but never wet.
5. Do not bend or cut off foliage when flowering is over. Leave it to die back naturally and provide the food needed for next year's flowers. If you have naturalised bulbs in a lawn, make sure they are a variety which are over before the lawn needs mowing.
6. Use only firm, fat bulbs which have a pleasant smell.
7. If you want earlier flowers, plant less than the usual depth of one to three times the size of the bulb.
8. In warm areas chill tulip bulbs before planting.
9. Bulbs may fail to flower if they are growing in shade, are overcrowded or if the previous year's foliage was cut off as soon as flowering was over. Very small bulbs need time before they can flower.

Diseases

Bulbs are susceptible to bacterial soft rot which rots them at ground level if there is too much water around or unrotted organic matter touching them. Viral diseases carried by aphids cause leaves to show irregular pale green or yellow patterns. The bulbs will have to be destroyed. Get rid of the aphids which carry the disease.

NATIVE PLANTS

Native species are often more resistant to insect attack than imported plants; after all, native plants, pests and predators all evolved in the same environment.

Never destroy what you think of as a pest on sight. Think of a small number of pests as insurance. They make certain there are always a number of predators around, and the number of those predators should build up as the pest numbers build up and will help to control them. When using an insecticide you are in danger of destroying more predators than pests.

Pick off pests by hand, use traps, suffocating oil or a diluted ash spray before you turn to an insecticide. Even organic controls are toxic to some degree — otherwise they would not kill. Fortunately they break down quickly and the residue is not toxic, unlike many conventional sprays.

If you must spray, use an organic insecticide and spray every second plant; wait three days, then spray the rest. This way you keep a small population of both pests and predators and the natural control system is not destroyed.

The nectar-eating birds you see hovering over the banksia and grevilleas prey on moths, borers and sawfly. Clerid beetles, lacewings, hoverflies and certain wasps which love native trees and blossom are very useful predators.

Common pests which attack native plants

Aphids

Aphids can be differently coloured but they all suck the sap of leaves, which wilt or become distorted. Sooty mould grows on the honeydew they secrete and they transfer viral diseases.

Grease-band the base of shrubs. Plant marigolds beneath trees. Encourage the natural predators — ladybirds and their larvae, lacewings, hoverflies and birds. Jet the pests off the plants with water or use a spray of diluted clay. Garlic, rhubarb leaf or lantana sprays can be used as a last resort . See **Recipes for pest and disease control**, p.137. Woolly aphids can be treated in the same way; you can also dab them with methylated spirits or squash them between thumb and fingers.

Beetles

Since beetles are voracious predators of other pests, make certain they are really damaging the plants before taking any action. Christmas beetles are large, shiny-winged insects that appear in summer and are often found struggling on their backs. They have large white grubs with reddish heads. The grubs eat plant roots; the beetles chew the leaves.

Strongly scented trees like lemon-scented gum seem less attractive to Christmas beetles but they are not immune from attack.

Shake the tree and stamp on all fallen beetles. Spray leaves with derris, pyrethrum or garlic. *See* **Recipes for pest and disease control**, p.137.

Borers

The larvae of several beetles and moths tunnel their way into stems and roots and do damage that is not apparent until a branch dies and the larvae are long gone. Look for deposits of sawdust around the base of trees and shrubs. Sickly trees are more prone to borer attack; if the tree is healthy the borer can become engulfed in resin as it burrows.

The moths do not seem to like the scent of lavender, nor will the females lay their eggs in trees that have had the trunk and main branches treated with bordeaux paste in a dilution of one to four. A thin slurry of wood ash painted on the wood of the tree will help to keep them away. If things become desperate try this strong repellent:
Soften 7 kg of soap in 4 litres of water for a few days. Heat it until it is too hot for the fingers; add ½ kg flour and 3½ kg naphthalene flakes; increase heat and stir until ingredients are dissolved. Apply warm with a paintbrush. Cool and store in an airtight container. Since this is not an organic remedy, you might care to replace the naphthalene flakes with oil of lavender, which is a good insect repellent, but it would be very expensive.

Caterpillars

Their natural predators — birds, wasps, mantids and centipedes — should all be encouraged. You can pick them off by hand or dust them with powdered clay which will dehydrate them or, in bad infestations, spray with derris, garlic or Dipel. *See* **Recipes for pest and disease control**, p.137.

Fern weevils

Fern weevils eat their way into stems and pupate in them. Cut out and burn infested stems or keep them under water for three weeks to kill the larvae.

Gall wasps

Some people find the galls created by the larvae of the gall wasps, or the parasite of the larvae, ugly and cut them out, though they rarely do trees any harm and rosellas, black cockatoos and other native birds eat them.

Kurrajong leaf-roller

This dull green caterpillar rolls leaves over and mats them together. The moth is yellow with black markings. Use derris or pyrethrum spray while the caterpillars are young. Try Dipel.

Mole crickets

These dull brown insects about 6 mm long have black eyes and strong front legs. They may uproot young plants and seedlings but since they usually cause minimal damage, why try to get rid of them?

If absolutely necessary, inject an emulsion of equal parts soft soap and eucalyptus oil into their tunnels in the soil or spread it thickly on the ground around the plant you wish to protect.

Psyllids

Psyllids have a wide range of predators and there is little need to take action against them as the infestation rarely lasts too long. Look for rounded or flat bumps on leaves. The nymphs build lerps, lacy or fan-shaped structures, to shelter the larvae, which are sap-suckers.

Sawflies

Sawflies are wasps, not flies; they got their name from the shape of their egg-laying equipment. They skeletonise leaves and defoliate trees. Birds, especially cuckoo shrikes and yellow robins, wasps and ants are their natural predators, so encourage them.

The steel blue sawfly (*Perga affinus*) attacks eucalyptus. When disturbed they raise head and abdomen and eject a stinging yellowish fluid from their mouth — hence the nickname 'spitfire'. They are black, about 70 mm long, and cluster around a branch. They lay eggs in summer and autumn.

The larvae of the callitrus sawfly (*Zenarge turneri*) are about 10-20 cm long and green. The callistemon sawfly has a sword-like protuberance on the abdomen and feeds only on callistemon — but voraciously. The leaf-blister sawfly attacks eucalypts. They feed between the upper and lower surface of young eucalyptus leaves, which then appear blistered. The infestations usually last only a season or two and do not return for some years.

Since they cluster in branches, sawflies are easy to shake off. Use a rake to agitate the upper branches. Stamp on the fallen insects — but be sure to wear boots! You could import chickens to do the job for you. You could prune off the lower branches that are heavily infested. Try spraying with Dipel even though sawflies are not true caterpillars. This is a bacterial derivative which has to be eaten to be effective so, when you spray with it, spray the leaves, not the sawflies. Derris, pyrethrum sprays made with soapy water are effective, and so are garlic, elder, tomato leaf and rhubarb leaf sprays. *See* **Recipes for pest and disease control**, p.137.

Slaters

Slaters are flat, grey, many-legged insects which shelter during the day and feed on young plant shoots at night.

Place wet or dry baits, of one part pyrethrum to two parts flour, near wood heaps or rubbish piles where the slaters hide during the day.

Staghorn frond beetles

These are small round beetles with orange larvae about a fingertip in size. They tunnel into staghorn fronds and pupate there.

Cut off the affected fronds if necessary. If you squash the stem you will squash the larvae inside and so break the breeding cycle.

Termites (white ants)

As soon as you see a termite nest, dig it out whole and burn it if you can; otherwise pour boiling water over it and drench it with pyrethrum spray. If the termites have infested a tree, cut it down and burn it if the infestation is bad; if it is not too bad, cut out the affected wood and burn it. Seal the cuts with grafting wax. Always try not to injure a tree at the base of the trunk as the termites will enter through an opening.

Thrips

Use the control methods for aphids.

PROBLEMS		
Banksia	Symptoms:	Chewed leaves
	Cause:	Banksia moth, longicorn looper, grevillea looper, double-headed hawk moth
	Solution:	Spray with quassia, derris or Dipel.
	Symptoms:	Leaves webbed together
	Cause:	Macadamia twig girdler
	Solution:	Spray with derris, pyrethrum or Dipel.
Boronia	Symptoms:	Gradual dieback; bush is shaky in the ground
	Cause:	Root-rot
	Solution:	Keep the soil well drained. Mulch with a lime and phosphorus-free compost.
	Symptoms:	Plant dies
	Cause:	Soil too hot and dry
	Solution:	Always keep boronias well-mulched.
Bottlebrush (Callistemon)	Symptoms:	Failure to flower
	Cause:	Too little direct sunlight
	Solution:	Move the bush
	Symptoms:	Skeletonised leaves
	Cause:	Sawfly
	Solution:	*See* **Sawflies**, p.124.
	Symptoms:	Brown spots on leaves
	Cause:	Brown spot; bush has too much shade
	Solution:	Spray with chamomile tea after rain or after watering; but if the bush is in the wrong place this will not solve the problem.
	Symptoms:	Galls on stems
	Cause:	Gall wasps
	Solution:	*See* **Gall wasps**, p.123.

PROBLEMS		
Bottlebrush (Callistemon) (continued)	Symptoms: Cause: Solution:	Leaf curl Thrips *See* **Roses**
	Symptoms: Cause: Solution:	Dead or dying branches, sawdust deposits at base of tree Moth borers *See* **Borers**, p.123.
Brush box	Symptoms: Cause: Solution:	Distorted new growth; powdery white wax on leaves Psyllids Use a soapy water spray. *See* **Psyllids** p.123.
	Symptoms: Cause: Solution:	Yellow spots on leaves Fungal leaf spot Spray with bordeaux in severe cases.
Cabbage tree	Symptoms: Cause: Solution:	Damaged young leaves at centre of the plant Cabbage tree moth Cut off dead leaves under which moths rest. Spray with white pepper, derris, pyrethrum or Dipel.
Christmas bush	Symptoms: Cause: Solution:	Dieback of top branches or whole bush *Phytophthora* root-rot Plant bushes only in well-drained soil. Protect bush from wind which will rock it and loosen the roots. If tree is affected, cut it back severely and keep fed with a foliar spray during recuperation. Keep soil liberally dressed with compost. Do not dig soil near bush and do not overwater.
Eucalypts	Symptoms: Cause: Solution:	Chewed leaves White-stemmed gum moth. These large, hairy moths with wavy, grey-brown marking on the wings have larvae about 110 mm long long with spiky tufts of hair. They rest behind the bark during the day and feed on the leaves at night. Wrap some sacking around the tree to provide it with daytime protection, then squash the moths.

PROBLEMS

Eucalypts (continued)	Symptoms: Cause: Solution:	Chewed leaves Eucalyptus and other weevils Wasps and other predators parasitise their eggs and so help to keep the weevils under control. Do not use sprays which would eliminate the wasps.
	Symptoms: Cause: Solution:	Clusters of grubs on leaves Sawflies *See* **Sawflies**, p.124.
	Symptoms: Cause: Solution:	Chewed leaves; trees can be defoliated Christmas beetles *See* **Beetles**, p.122.
	Symptoms: Cause: Solution:	Dead or dying branches, sawdust deposits at base of tree Borers *See* **Borers**, p.123.
	Symptoms: Solution:	Mistletoe growing on a tree Cut off only if it seems to be harming the tree. There are mistletoes that parasitise other mistletoes.
	Symptoms: Cause: Solution:	Scribbly marks on the bark Scribbly gum moth Enjoy the designs; the moth does no harm to the tree.
Geebung	Symptoms: Cause: Solution:	Brown spots on leaves Leaf-spot Do not plant tree in shade. Use chamomile, casuarina or garlic spray. Do not overwater.
Geraldton wax	Symptoms: Cause: Solution:	Wilted or yellow leaves; dieback *Phytophthora* root-rot Plant only in sandy, well-drained soil in a sunny position. Do not disturb by digging around the bush and do not mulch. Keep other plants away.

PROBLEMS		
Grevillea	Symptoms: Cause: Solution:	Encrustations on leaves Scale Grease-band the base to deter ants. Spray with white oil if the temperature is under 24°C. Spray with soapy water at any time.
	Symptoms: Cause: Solution:	Chewed leaves Caterpillars Sprinkle white pepper on leaves. Spray with either Dipel, bug juice, garlic or pyrethrum.
	Symptoms: Cause: Solution:	Dead or dying branches; sawdust deposits at base of tree Borers *See* **Borers**, p.123.
	Symptoms: Cause: Solution:	Brown spots on leaves Leaf-spot fungus Improve air circulation around bush; wipe foliage clean with a kitchen cloth dipped in chive or chamomile tea. Spray with casuarina or bordeaux in cool weather or late in the evening.
Hakea	Symptoms: Cause: Solution:	Black spots on leaves Fungal leaf-spot Improve drainage and access to sunlight. Spray with elder, chives, chamomile, half strength bordeaux in winter.
Kurrajong flame tree	Symptoms: Cause: Solution:	Dying branches; tunnels in the wood; sawdust deposits Kurrajong weevil *See* **Borers**, p.123.
	Symptoms: Cause: Solution:	Chewed leaves Kurrajong leaf moth Dust leaves with white pepper. Use garlic, quassia or Dipel spray.

PROBLEMS

Lillypilly	Symptoms:	Small scales and sooty mould on leaves
	Cause:	Scale
	Solution:	Use a white oil spray when the temperature is under 24°C. Otherwise spray with soapy water and pyrethrum and if the problem continues, garlic, quassia or pyrethrum spray.
Melaleuca	Symptoms:	Chewed leaves; pupae in bark
	Cause:	Paperbark sawfly
	Solution:	*See* **Sawflies**, p.124.
	Symptoms:	New shoots die back
	Cause:	Fungal dieback
	Solution:	Cut off affected shoots; spray with casuarina or bordeaux in cool weather.
Mint bush (*Prostanthera*)	Symptoms:	Bushes are spindly
	Solution:	Tip prune bush each year when young; thereafter, prune after flowering is over.
	Symptoms:	Dieback
	Cause:	*Phytophthora* root-rot
	Solution:	Plant mint bushes only in well-drained soil, preferably gravelly. Mulch with compost but keep it away from the stem. Water carefully; do not allow soil to become saturated. Buy a bush which has been grafted on to Coast Rosemary (*Westringia fruticosa*) which is resistant to root-rot.

Norfolk Island pine The progressive dieback of these trees on beachfronts is said to be caused by sewage pollutants containing detergents blowing back on to the land.

Photinia	Symptoms:	Small scales and sooty mould on leaves
	Cause:	Scale
	Solution:	Grease-band tree trunk to deter ants. Spray with white oil if temperature is under 24°C. Spray with soapy water at any time but be careful — the spray could damage the flowers.

PROBLEMS		
Photinia (continued)	Symptoms: Cause: Solution:	Small insects clustered around shoots Aphids Jet pests off with water. Use either dilute clay, wormwood, garlic, or rhubarb leaf spray. Use pyrethrum or derris spray as a last resort.
	Symptoms: Cause: Solution:	Powdery deposits on leaves Powdery mildew Spray with milk, garlic or chamomile, if necessary, with half strength bordeaux in the cool of the evening.
Pittosporum	Symptoms: Cause: Solution:	Small scales on plant; possible sooty mould Scale Use oil spray if temperature is under 24°C. Otherwise use a dilute clay spray or soapy water with or without pyrethrum.
	Symptoms: Cause: Solution:	Small, pale, slightly dimpled specks on leaves Leaf-miner Disfiguration is slight and damage rarely enough to affect the vigour of the tree so ignore it.
	Symptoms: Cause: Solution:	Young leaves are curled Thrips Some thrips are useful predators and eat mites or aphids. Don't destroy unless they are really damaging your plants. Hope for rain or hot dry weather to reduce numbers; encourage wasps, bugs, spiders, fungi, ladybirds, lacewings and other natural controls. Otherwise try strong jets of preferably hot water, dilute clay spray, a soapy water spray, onion or derris spray.
Tea tree (*Leptospermum*)	Symptoms: Cause: Solution:	Chewed leaves, mass of webs Tea-tree web moth Remove webs and burn them; spray with either pyrethrum or garlic in soapy water.

PROBLEMS

Tea Tree (continued)	Symptoms:	Sooty mould on leaves
	Cause:	Scale
	Solution:	Wipe leaves clean with a kitchen cloth. Use a chamomile spray after scales have been removed.
Waratah (*Telopea*)	Symptoms:	Failure to flower
	Solution:	Since the tree flowers on terminal shoots, prune regularly to encourage more growth.
Wattle (*Acacia*)	Symptoms:	Dieback
	Cause:	Old age
	Solution:	Cutting back to good wood may prolong the life of the tree.
	Symptoms:	Thin line or pink blister on leaves
	Cause:	Larvae of the wattle leaf-miner
	Solution:	Cut off and burn affected leaves. Spray with pyrethrum in soapy water. Unfortunately, this may not be effective.
	Symptoms:	Galls on stems; lumps on leaves
	Cause:	Gall wasps
	Solution:	Cut off and burn galls on stems. Do the same with affected leaves. There is no point in spraying as the larvae of the wasp are out of reach.
	Symptoms:	Oval insects about 4 mm long, purple-black with white wax stripes, feeding on soft new growth
	Cause:	Wattle mealy bugs
	Solution:	Prune off affected shoots if it seems necessary. Harm is likely to be minimal.
	Symptoms:	Blue-grey to dark brown large scale insects about 5 mm across on leaves and stems. They can be dull or shiny and are usually grouped together.
	Solution:	They will probably be cleared by their predators; if they are not, pick them off by hand or spray them with garlic in soapy water.

PROBLEMS		
Wattle (Acacia) (continued)	Symptoms:	Froth on leaves and stems
	Cause:	Spittlebugs
	Solution:	The froth is produced by nymphs as a protection. Though the adults are sap-suckers they do little damage. Hose them off the tree.
	Symptoms:	Streaky brown spots on leaves. Leaves may die.
	Cause:	Acacia spotting bug
	Solution:	Spray with either derris or pyrethrum in soapy water.
Waxflower	Symptoms:	Small scales on leaves and stems
	Cause:	White wax scale
	Solution:	Leave alone unless plant is suffering. Use a light oil spray, avoiding the flowers, if the temperature is under 24°C, a soapy water spray in the cool of the evening, or a quassia or garlic spray at any time.

LAWNS

Five steps to a healthy lawn

Choose the right grass for your needs.

Do not buy seed because it is cheap or immediately available. Inspect lawns in the area — in both summer and winter — and get local advice. The following list will give an idea of the various grasses you could grow.

Bent grass. Cool to cold climate.
Needs moist, cool conditions and will not tolerate drought, heatwave or hard wear. Some shade and salt tolerance; suitable for coastal areas.

Buffalo grass. Warm to hot climate.
Will tolerate dry conditions if not too prolonged or the weather too hot, but will not tolerate shade. Fairly hard-wearing.

Chamomile. Cool to warm climate.
The Treneague strain needs no mowing and never flowers. Other chamomiles must be mown. Will take short dry spells but cannot stand long hot ones.

Clover. Cool to warm climate.
Tolerates some salt, drought and shade. White clover will not tolerate shade, salt or hard wear. Needs plenty of water.

Couch. Warm to hot climate.
Reasonably drought and salt-tolerant. Dislikes shade. Loses colour in winter in warm areas.

Dichondra. Cold to hot climate.
Drought-tolerant. Will also thrive in moist conditions. Needs shade in very hot areas and will not tolerate salt or hard wear. A creeping grass which makes excellent cover between paving stones but can be invasive.

Fescues. Cool to cold climate.
Reasonably drought-resistant and hard-wearing. Tolerates shade. Makes good spring growth and keeps its colour in winter.

Kentucky blue grass. Cool to cold climate.
Some drought and broken shade tolerance. Cannot take salt in the air.

Kikuyu. Warm to hot climate.
Hard-wearing; drought and salt-tolerant. Hates shade. Very invasive.

Lawn thyme. Cold to hot climate.
Hard-wearing; drought-tolerant; does not mind broken shade and poor soil. Some varieties have fragrant pink or white flowers which are less fragrant in moist conditions. It is prickly to sit on.

Lucerne. Cool to hot climate.
An excellent alternative to grass. A deep-rooting plant which gives several cuttings of nitrogen-rich mulch a year. It is drought-tolerant once established and fixes nitrogen in the soil. It becomes more closely matted the more it is cut.

Perennial rye. Cool to cold climate.
Don't use it if you are prone to sinus trouble or hay fever. Hard-wearing and thick-matting lawn that is shade-tolerant. Fair drought

133

tolerance once established. Will tolerate mildly salty conditions.

Phylla nodiflora. Cool to hot climate.
Needs full sun. Won't take hard wear until established. Attracts bees. May need mowing.

Choose the site carefully

Grass dislikes heavy shade and exposed dry areas.

Mow regularly

Mow as soon as there has been about 3 mm of new growth. Different grasses should be cut at different heights. Couch is best cut at 15 mm; kikuyu at about 20 mm, and coarser, warm-climate grasses do best at around 40 mm. Do not be tempted to cut too short; longer grass has longer roots and is better able to forage for moisture and nutrients. Never cut more than a third off the height of the grass at any one time. Do not mow when the temperature is over 35°C. Wait until the cool of the evening and water immediately afterwards. Do not attempt to mow wet grass — you'll tear it.

Fertilise carefully

A little blood and bone scattered over the lawn in early spring will supply the phosphorus needed to help to keep the grass green and able to hold moisture. You can sprinkle fine compost over the lawn at anytime. Leave clippings on the lawn to add as food and to supply humus, but rake and spread them evenly.

Water regularly

Grass is relatively shallow-rooted so there is no need to water heavily. Too much water often creates humidity and with that comes mildew and fungal problems which can spread to the rest of the garden. Dig a test hole and see how long it takes water to reach the roots and then water, just enough and no more, twice a week.

Problems

A vigorous, well-fed and well-watered lawn will be able to withstand and outgrow pest problems. If you have dry patches, sprinkle the lawn with compost and leave the mown grass as a mulch but spread it out evenly. If you have green, slimy patches or irregular green to brown-orange patches of algae, improve the drainage. Is the lawn in too much shade? If it is you could replace the grass with a shade-tolerant ground cover. If your grass seed has a poor germination rate, mix it with sand and fine grass clippings when you sow. The sand will help to spread it evenly and the clippings will shelter it. Dog and cat urine can kill lawn grass. Sprinkle your pets' favourite spots with pepper. As soon as you see the tell-tale circle of yellowing grass, soak it with water.

Lawn weeds

Weeds will grow where the lawn grass is not thick enough, drainage is poor, tree roots are invading the soil and the feeding regime is poor. Feed and mow regularly. Dig out weeds with a sharp trowel — which can be attached to a long stick if you do not feel like stooping — or use a nylon brush cutter.

You can paint weeds with kerosene or petrol. Do not use weed killers as they could be a danger to children playing on the lawn or to anyone who likes the feel of grass under the bare feet. Sulphate of ammonia can be used for general control. Sprinkle it over the grass when it is wet with dew and water it in. The disadvantage is that it will kill clover, which can be valuable as a nitrogen-fixer and protein enricher of the soil. It is not organic. An organic weed-killer is human urine saved for a few days until it starts to smell like ammonia. Pour it carefully over the weeds and do not water the lawn for a few days.

Bindii eyes

These small barbed plants should be dug out in winter when they show up against the darker green of the lawn. Alternatively, treat them with sulphate of ammonia or undiluted urine.

Oxalis

The pink flowers with clover-like leaves and thin stems are all too familiar. Dig out the underground bulbs in winter when food reserves are low. Perseverence now is well worthwhile.

Paspalum

This has a tough, woody crown that can be easily severed by a swipe with the mattock. Fortunately, the roots left in the soil will not regenerate.

LAWN PESTS AND DISEASES	
Symptoms:	Patches of grass chewed off at ground level. The grass dies.
Cause:	Black-headed pasture cockchafer (white curl grubs)
Solution:	Pour a soapy rhubarb or pyrethrum spray down the holes. Improve feeding. Cockchafers lay their eggs in sparse grass. If the problem proves intractable, try another grass species.
Symptoms:	Grass stalk chewed through at ground level
Cause:	Cutworms
Solution:	Drench the lawn with a one-in-10 solution of molasses and water. This will dehydrate the worms. Leave a pile of old leaves on the lawn as a trap; remove and squash trapped worms. Keep up the organic matter in the soil, especially in sandy areas.
Symptoms:	Bare patches, especially in autumn and winter
Cause:	Corbies
Solution:	Spray with Dipel at night. Make a trap using port-wine. *See* **Codling moth** pp.88-90
Symptoms:	Rotted slimy grass when nights are cold and weather wet
Cause:	Fusarium patch
Solution:	Add potash to the soil and keep the compost component high.
Symptoms:	Poor-looking grass in a couch lawn
Cause:	Couch root-rot
Solution:	Drench with chamomile or casuarina tea and keep well fed. If no response, try another grass species — the disease is specific to couch.

LAWN PESTS AND DISEASES

Symptoms:	Thin straggly grass with oval, cottony insects on stems
Cause:	Grass crown mealy bug
Solution:	Keep grass growing well and cut frequently. The bug has a waxy coat sprays cannot penetrate, but try an oil spray in cool weather or a derris or pyrethrum spray at any time.
Symptoms:	Bleached circles in the grass and fine webbing. Silvery mites are just visible.
Cause:	Grass-webbing mites and other mites
Solution:	Spray affected patches with a soapy pyrethrum, derris or rhubarb leaf mixture. The milder sprays, anise and coriander, can also help.
Symptoms:	Slow-growing grass. Clouds of small insects rise when grass is walked on
Cause:	Couchtip maggot
Solution:	Spray the grass thoroughly with Dipel but do not water it in. If this fails, use pyrethrum and water it in.
Symptoms:	Pale grass with bare circles; deformed and twisted new shoots; short, brownish roots; condition is worse in humid weather.
Cause:	Damping off
Solution:	The condition is worse in lawns which have been given a high-nitrogen boost. Add some ground rock phosphate now and stick to compost, blood and bone and a very thin scattering of old hen manure or other dried manure in future. Try watering the lawn liberally with chamomile tea.
Symptoms:	Rusty-looking grass
Cause:	Rust
Solution:	Cut grass regularly and dust it with dried hen manure or blood and bone.

RECIPES FOR PEST AND DISEASE CONTROL

You can grow most of the ingredients needed in the following recipes or buy them at a health food store. Soap can be added to all the recipes as a 'sticking' agent but, if you wish to store a spray, it will keep better without.

All-purpose spray

To be used as a last resort. Mix 1 part pyrethrum *or* derris *or* nicotine *or* rhubarb leaf spray with one part garlic *or* elder *or* lilac spray. Add two parts nettle *or* chamomile *or* chives spray.

Anise spray

For use against thrips. Pour boiling water on anise seeds and steep until the water is pale brown. Use fresh. Do not store.

Azalea spray

Mix together equal parts garlic, chamomile and nettle 'tea' and spray bushes thoroughly, once a week, covering the underside of the leaves. This spray will help to both prevent and cure most of the ills to which azaleas are heir.

Baking soda spray

This is a fungicide and is not strictly organic. It can be used instead of bordeaux and is slightly easier to make. Never let the spray touch the foliage or flowers. Use at once. Do not store. Mix 100 grams washing soda with 50 grams soft soap. Dilute with two litres water.

Bordeaux

This is the standard organic fungicide. Always make your own; the commercial mixtures are not traditional bordeaux. Try not to use bordeaux too often as the copper in it can affect soil fungi and kill beneficial predators. It is useful against scale and, to a lesser extent, mites.

Mix 90 grams blue copper sulphate with 4 ½ litres of water in a non-metallic container. In another non-metallic container, mix 125 grams slaked lime — this is bricklayers' lime, not agricultural — with 4 ½ litres cold water. Mix the two together and stir well.

Dip an old nail into the mixture and keep it there for 30 seconds. If it turns blue you either need more lime or have not dissolved the lime sufficiently. Do not use the mixture until the nail is unaffected, otherwise you would burn the plants if you sprayed them with the mixture. Use within the hour. Stir occasionally or it will separate. The mixture can clog the nozzles of the spray gun so keep water on hand to wash them out.

Bordeaux paste

This is useful for collar-rot and tree wounds. Dissolve 60 grams copper sulphate in 2 litres of water, then add 120 grams of bricklayer's lime mixed in two litres of water. A tablespoon of powdered skim milk will help.

Bug juice

Mash up pests in a mortar and pestle or a blender and cover with water. Stand for a while then strain. Mix 1 cc of the juice with 20 litres water. For some pests like scale you can use the leaves to which they are attached as well. You will need less water.

Casuarina

A mild fungicide and an excellent preventative

spray for fungal bacterial and mildew problems. Make a tea of 8-9 grams casuarina needles to 1 litre of boiling water.

Chamomile

Chamomile tea is a mild fungicide. Pour boiling water over a handful of chamomile flowers to make a 'tea' or use a bought teabag according to instructions on the packet. Leave to steep for 10 minutes, strain and use liquid as a spray when cool. The liquid should be a weak tea colour.

Chives

As for chamomile.

Clay

Mix clay with water and use as thick a mix as possible to suffocate aphids and other pests.

Condy's crystals (Permanganate of potash)

Good for powdery mildew. Dissolve 7 grams potassium permanganate in 7 litres of water. Use immediately.

Coriander

Effective against red spider mites and woolly aphids. Boil one part coriander leaves in one part water for 10 minutes. Strain and spray. Coriander is often used mixed with anise.

Derris

The spray is a general insecticide but breaks down under sunlight after a few days and spraying must be repeated. It is deadly to fish, so do not spray near tanks or ponds. It is not an effective contact poison and works best when ingested, so spray the leaves and not the pests.

Mix 120 grams soap with 4 ½ litres of water. Mix 60 grams derris dust with 4 ½ litres af water. Combine the two and add 12 litres of water. If it separates, remix.

Dipel

This is a commercially available bacteria, *Bacillus thuringiensis*, used against caterpillars, pear and cherry slugs and others.

Elder

This all-purpose but weak insecticide is a fungicide too and is effective against mildew and black spot. Boil 500 grams elder leaves in a litre of water in a closed pan. Top up water as necessary. Try not to inhale the steam. Strain and use when cool. Label **poison** and store in a dark place.

Garlic

Garlic is an effective fungicide and insecticide and should be used with care to avoid wiping out beneficial predators. Chop up 85 grams unpeeled garlic and leave to soak in two tablespoonsful mineral oil for 24 hours. Dissolve 7 grams soap in 600 ml water. Mix with the soaked garlic. Strain. Store in glass, *not metal*, away from the light. Keep out of the reach of children. Use diluted in a one-to-10 water solution. If that is not effective, use a stronger mix. The smell is not bad and does not linger after spraying. See also onion- garlic spray.

Glue

A weak solution of flour and water will suffocate small insects and their eggs, particularly aphids and thrips. The solution flakes off when dry.

Horseradish

Fill any sized container full of finely chopped horseradish leaves. Cover with boiling water and leave standing for 48 hours. Use diluted in a one-to-4 water solution.

Horsetail (Equisetum)

Use to prevent fungal, bacterial and mildew problems. Cut off all infected leaves and spray the rest to stop infection spreading.

Boil 20 grams leaves in a litre of water for half an hour. Strain. Use one litre of spray to cover an area 10 metres by 10 metres, and use at 50 per cent strength for a subsequent spraying. You will not achieve better control by using a stronger concentrate.

Insect repellent spray

Mix chopped garlic and onion, lavender leaves

and flowers, mint and yarrow and cover with water. Stand in a closed container for 24 hours. Strain. Add an equal quantity of water and a few drops of detergent and use as a plant spray.

Lantana

Lantana spray is effective against aphids. Boil 500 grams leaves in a litre of water for a time. Strain and use when cool.

Lilac

Lilac leaves and berries are poisonous. Take care using the spray and, if you must store it, make sure to label the bottle **poison**. The spray is a useful fungicide and a mild general insecticide.

Boil one part of leaves in three parts of water for half an hour — but *not* in the family stewpot — and take care not to inhale the fumes. Strain. Use as a spray when cool.

Milk

Milk is effective against a range of mildews, mites and other pests. Use equal parts milk and water and spray every few days until mildews disappear.

Nettle

Nettle spray is effective against aphids and makes a good general tonic spray. Boil some nettles in enough water to cover them for 10 minutes. Dilute water until weak tea colour. Strain and use spray when cool.

Nicotine

Use nicotine spray only as a last resort. It is useful against any pest. It breaks down quickly.

Boil 56 grams cigarette or pipe tobacco in 2 ¼ litres water for 30 minutes. Strain. Dilute with four times the amount of water to one part mixture. Add 20 grams soapflakes to each litre and dissolve well. The spray will keep for several weeks but slowly loses effectiveness. Make sure bottles are labelled **poison**. Do not spray within seven days of harvest.

Oil

Oil sprays suffocate insects and their eggs, and are most effective in winter when the insect is most porous. Do not use an oil spray if the temperature is higher than 24ºC.

Heat a kilogram of soap in 8 litres of oil and stir until soap is thoroughly dissolved. Keep this mixture on hand and when you use it, mix the chosen quantity with 20 times its volume of water. If you mix it with water and store it, it will separate.

Onion

Onion spray is good against scale, thrip, aphids and mites. Pour boiling water over a kilo of chopped, unpeeled onions to cover. Allow to stand. Strain. Dilute with 20 litres water. Spray every 10 days until pests are gone.

Onion and garlic

Effective against most leaf-eating insects, this spray even has a limited use against hard-bodied ones like shield bugs. Try it before you move on to anything stronger.

Chop up four hot chillies, four large onions and two cloves of garlic. Cover with soapy water and leave to steep for 24 hours. Strain and add 2 litres of water. Sealed and stored in a dark place, the container will keep for up to two weeks.

Parsnip

Use against pea aphids and red spider mites. Chop up some roots and leave, covered with water, in a sealed container overnight. Strain; add an equal quantity of water and use.

Pyrethrum (Feverfew)

This is a good general insecticide spray which is harmless to animals and human beings. Its effect is not long-lasting; it breaks down in sunlight in from two hours to two days. Use it in the evenings so that it will not kill bees. It can be made from pulverised pyrethrum flowers, *Chrysanthemum cinerariaefolium* or from feverfew flowers which are incorrectly called pyrethrum. You will need to use double the quantity of feverfew flowers.

Steep one tablespoonful pyrethrum powder or two tablespoonsful dried flowers in hot, soapy water for an hour. You could use plain water but the soap helps the spray to stay on the plant. Do not be tempted to boil the pyrethrum in the water; the fumes are toxic.

Quassia

The spray makes a weak general insecticide. Boil 56 grams quassia chips in 6 litres water for two hours. Strain. Add enough soap to make a lather. Allow to cool before use. Quassia chips are available at most health food stores.

Rhubarb

A spray made from rhubarb leaves is harmless to bees and breaks down quickly, but it is harmful to human beings. Be sure to keep it out of the reach of children.

Boil 1 kilogram in 3 litres of water for half an hour. Strain. Add some soap. Dilute with equal quantity of water before spraying.

Ryania

Ryania is successful overseas against caterpillars, beetles and codling moth, but in harsh Australian conditions it is less so. It is harmless to most of our native predators.

Mix 100 grams ryania powder with 10 litres soapy water. Spray every 10 to 14 days.

Sugar

Drenching the soil with a sugar solution will dehydrate the nematodes in it. You could use molasses instead of sugar — but *never* use honey, which could tansmit diseases to bees. Use sparingly. Most nematodes are not pests and too much sugar will harm the soil. To make the solution, dissolve 2 kilograms sugar or molasses in a bucket of water.

Sulphur

Sulphur is effective for mites and scale but may burn new shoots, flowers and tender foliage. Sulphur should be applied in a Bordeaux mixture with lime, lightly dusted or in a one-to-three water solution (or as directed by the manufacturer). As a pest control apply sulphur in late spring or early winter.

Tomato

A spray made from tomato leaves is toxic to human beings and a general insecticide.

Boil 1 kilogram tomato leaves in 1 litre water for 30 minutes. Mix enough soapy water to make a lather. Use when cool. Do not store.

Turnip

This kills pea aphids, red spider mites and flies.

Chop up roots and cover with water. Leave to steep overnight in a covered container. Strain. Add an equal quantity of soapy water and spray.

Urine

Human urine is very effective against a range of mildews as well as apple and pear scab. It is sterile unless the donor has a urinary tract infection but doesn't remain sterile if stored, and will develop a strong odour. Use fresh.

Washing soda and soap

This spray controls scale and aphids.

Dissolve 250 grams washing soda in ½ litre boiling water. Grate soap and add it to the mixture. Heat until dissolved. Add 13½ litres cold water. Stir until mixed. Use at once. Do not store.

Willow-water

Tightly pack any sized container with chopped, pliable willow stalks. Cover with boiling water and allow to stand for 48 hours. Use as an undiluted spray.

Wormwood

Aphids and snails dislike wormwood, which is useful to spray around seedlings .

Cover leaves with boiling water and leave to steep for three hours. Strain and use with one part solution to four parts plain water.

INDEX

141

143